THE CRICKE
HIRST, AND S

EDITOR: E. F. BENSON, EUSTACE MILES

Published by

Design and setting By Zinc Read
Email- zincread@gmail.com
ISBN-978-93-6776-245-5

CONTENTS

CHAPTER I.

BATTING AND RUNNING.

I.--INTRODUCTORY.

IT was once thought that the universe moved round our earth merely as its accompanying condition, existing simply and solely for the sake of our earth. And so the batsman has been, and generally still is, regarded as the centre of cricket, for whose enjoyment the rest of the players subsist. Batting seems best worth while, not so much because of the qualities, such as pluck, which it demands, as because of the pleasure it may give. The reason why most people like batting, even if they hate wicket-keeping and fielding and watching, and do not bowl, is the enjoyment of striking and of scoring runs. Perhaps in this there is some relic of the desire for hitting and killing--the desire for overcoming and controlling Nature, for using power. Moreover, batting includes defence as well as attack; indeed the safest defence may really be to attack boldly. Batting at its best and fullest involves a complexity of characteristics: it involves back-play, with gliding and late cutting, pulling, forward play, with the cut-drive and ordinary drive, the "half-cock" stroke, the snick; a decision between these varieties, followed by a hit, then recovery of balance, then a decision whether one shall run or not, then perhaps a run, then a turn at the crease--and much besides this. It may involve a great change of habit. Thus in many other ball-games the ball is hit when it is further off from the striker's foot--as in Golf, Racquets, Tennis, Lawn Tennis, Fives. In Cricket, except in such strokes as the pull and the cut, the ball should be hit when it is near to the striker's foot.

He who is not born a batsman, he who wishes to be made--that is, make himself--an all-round batsman, must learn not only general rules like this, but also details with regard to the individual strokes. In studying these details he will meet divergent theories; here again is scope for individual trial and judgment, and for observation. He can notice what the best players actually *do*, for, as Murdoch says, this is of more importance than what they think they do.

The would-be batsman, therefore, is offered perhaps a few really universal laws, and certainly many general hints, yet he must judge of each hint by its results in his own case after fair experiment. He must be a free agent. He may find that the advisers have assumed that he has little reach, little activity, whereas he may be a Ford or Abel for reach, a Jessop or Abel for activity, without the safety of a Shrewsbury or the strength of a Hirst. Why should such a one be tied down by a law that in forward play he shall not let his bat pass beyond his left foot, if he has it in his power to send his bat with force many inches beyond that point, and so smother the ball? Who shall bind down such players? On the other hand, who shall spoil the slow player's pleasure and safety by bidding him run out?

Throughout this chapter all rules or hints are submitted to the test of utility for the individual. They must be studied; questions must be asked of coaches and others, who should explain strokes by doing them; the mechanisms must be found out, and also the causes and reasons for them. These mechanisms--some will be described later on--must be mastered, if not in early life, then now; they must be mastered sensibly, not with huge bats and balls to begin with, but with lighter implements. The advice must all be judged by its effects.

If the reader will bear in mind that the mechanisms suggested, together with the other helps, are not necessarily the best (though they are based on a study of what the best players actually do in games), he will treat them in the right spirit, with a view to sensible trial and judgment by fruits. Anyhow, be these helps right or wrong, it is obvious that, by all except the genius player, *some* A B C should be acquired as a personal possession and habit before much regular play has confirmed bad habits. Mr. Edward Lyttelton insists on this in the following passage, after he has described what is needed for a correct stroke:--

"Now from these principles, which some might call truisms, a very important practical maxim proceeds. All sound rules of batting should be practised by a young cricketer without the ball as well as with it. The grammar of the science can be partly learnt in the bedroom; the application of the rules must be made on the green sward. Many a finished batsman has tried this plan. Five minutes devoted every night by an aspiring cricketer to a leg hit, or cut, or forward play at a phantom ball, will gradually discipline his sinews to the required posture, besides sending him to bed in a right frame of mind.

"I think it was Harry Jupp who used to ascribe his astonishingly good defence to a habit of this kind. He used to place a large-sized mirror on the floor--not for purposes of personal vanity--but to see if the bat moved in a straight line. To make the test better, a line was drawn along the floor from the centre of the mirror, along which line the bat was to move.

The least deviation was then manifested, not only at the end of the stroke, but while it was being made."

2.--THE ALPHABET OF SAFE BATTING.

It is not part of the alphabet of *safe* batting to meet and attack the ball always. Both W. G. and C. B. Fry began their careers with safety, with the stopping of balls; afterwards they proceeded to splendid execution. The A B C of safe batting is not quite identical with the A B C of effective batting, which will be considered in subsequent sections of this chapter.

One of the first rules of safety is said to be to "keep the eye on the ball." This rule needs alteration.[2] Before the delivery the eye should watch the bowler's arm, wrist, and fingers; Shrewsbury owed to this observation of something besides the ball a long innings against the Australians many years ago. To foretell a change in direction, length, pace, break, etc., is not easy by the sight of the ball alone. It is after the ball has left the bowler's hand that it must be sedulously watched. Nor can it always be watched right on to the bat; exactly how far it can be watched is a much disputed point. Certainly few batsmen can carry out the golden rule of Golf. I believe that most of them--I speak from my own Tennis and Racquet experience--take their eyes off the cricket-ball too soon. Few err by looking at it too long. In my games, almost without exception, the longer I look at the ball the better my stroke is.

The second law is correct timing. There are several kinds of good sight; I doubt if any one of them by itself brings with it that desirable faculty, "the good eye." Ranjitsinhji and others rightly include, under the timing, the judgment as to the flight (direction, pace, etc.), the decision as to what is or is not to be done, the command that the best things shall be done, the correct combination and co-operation of the requisite parts at just the very moment.[3] I believe that the good eye, where it is not already a natural or acquired habit, means a splendidly accurate and therefore healthy working of a vast number of more or less separate nerve centres and nerves; but that what is often called "a good eye" is nothing of the sort--it is a mastery of certain correct mechanisms, which, if a man possesses them for his own, can produce an even better effect than the most superb eyesight without such mechanism. I may have a far better sight and eye for games than a fairly well-taught golfer who knows what muscles to use, and has these as half-automatic habits; but put me against him, and ask any spectators which of us has the better eye, and they will very likely point to my opponent.

If this be so, then the third rule will be *to have already secured* the best possible mechanisms, and to have made them easy and sub-conscious; at first perhaps they may be conquered one by one; in the end, however, they must be not independent units, but co-operating parts of a unit--members combining and working together in harmony, as in some businesses, adding power each to each, relieving one another. These mechanisms include, for many strokes, and especially the forward strokes, the "straight bat," i.e., the bat held straight and not sideways as it meets the ball; with its handle nearer to the bowler than its blade is; with the end of its blade just to the side of the left foot; the bat moving as straight as may be towards the approaching ball from start to finish (the finish being a follow-through after the ball has been struck); quickness of foot and leg to start and to move, the right leg being the base and pivot; the power to get right to the pitch of the ball or else to wait for it as far back as possible; straight and fast and full extensions of various limbs in various directions; a control of many different strokes, and especially, in these days of fast plumb-wickets, a control of the forward stroke. The reader will best realise the number of these mechanisms if we mention (and if he meanwhile realises by trial) *some* of those which are parts of the ordinary forward stroke:--the right leg straight and unbent, the right foot firm, the left foot and leg sent out towards the ball (a little to the left of the line of flight), the left elbow and wrist shot well forward at full stretch (in order to keep the ball down), the right shoulder forward and down, the bat moved straight down and towards the approaching ball and beyond it (not necessarily straight along the line between the wickets), the weight brought forward with the head of the bat, the recovery of balance and position, and the readiness to run directly after the ball has been struck or missed. If one has run out first, then the right foot will still have to serve as a firm pivot for the whole stroke, which must be a single movement. This will give some idea of what the correct mechanisms are, quite apart from individual peculiarities in the use of them. Such correct mechanisms may be acquired separately as I acquired my Tennis mechanisms, and as fencers acquire their fencing--mechanisms of lunge, wrist-play, etc.; but it is part of the A B C of correct play *to have already acquired them* as correct members of a correct whole before the game begins. Add to these the mechanisms and the combination of mechanisms for other strokes, such as back-play, cut, pull, etc., and the reader will agree that the A B C of batting is no light work for anyone, except the born player who apparently has not had to learn it letter by letter.

Out of the list of useful mechanisms a few will now be suggested. It is for the reader to judge how far they actually are used in the strokes of leading experts. Each example must be compared with the positions and movements of the best models, as shown in photographs like these, or in actual games or practice.

SOME SAMPLE EXERCISES.

Before attempting these exercises, the reader should find out the principles of correct practice, some of which are suggested in Chapter VIII. One or two of the most vital may be selected here.

(1.) Decide whether it is worth while to play Cricket at all; if so, whether it is worth while to improve your standard of skill; if so, whether these and your own exercises are likely to be of appreciable help. (The exercises are not meant to take the place of net-practice and games, which are indispensable, but to make them more pleasant and useful.)

(2.) During the exercises, concentrate your whole attention either upon the muscles at work, or upon their reflection in a looking-glass.

(3.) Aim at correctness, and therefore begin slowly and carefully before you repeat any given movement. Freedom, pace, endurance, strength will then increase almost of their own accord. Freedom and pace may best be acquired by movements done at first without implements, afterwards with light implements. I found these two preliminary stages invaluable in the preparation for my games, perhaps especially for the sharp movements of Racquets. The worst possible beginning is any "exerciser" that requires a tense grip.

(4.) In case of a fault (discovered by yourself or pointed out by others), seek to exaggerate the opposite fault.

Among the most useful exercises for batting, as for bowling and fielding, are the fast and full and straight extensions of various muscles and muscle-combinations, with economy of the unused parts, and without loss of, or with immediate recovery of, the body's balance, and readiness to be directed elsewhither. It is likely that these pages contain errors, but I think that if one were to ask a good player where he ached most of all after his first practice or game in the season, one would find that the aches were mainly due to these extension movements (of the latissimus dorsi, below and behind the arm-pit, etc.).

For the feet and legs, (i.) Lunge far forward (but not so far as to strain yourself) with the left foot and leg in a direct line (not a curve) in various directions (perhaps along various chalk lines upon the floor) with full weight--the head should come almost over the left foot--but with rapid recovery of balance.

(ii.) Start to run in the forward direction afterwards.

(iii.) Practise the position and movement for backing up and a quick start to run.

(iv.) Practise the movement for turning at the crease, as shown in the photograph of Shrewsbury.

For the neck. Move the head round, at first slowly and carefully, from side to side, then up and down, and so on; but do not strain.

For the trunk: the body's force is great, as--to use an old illustration--one can see when one bumps against a wall in the dark. (i.) The body-swing from the hips is a most useful movement. Keeping the legs as stiff as possible, and the head as still as possible, twist round the shoulders, first to the right, then to the left. (ii.) Bend the trunk forwards, and then sideways, from the hips.

For the shoulders, arm, and forearm. (i.) To the lunge of the left foot add an equally full and direct and fast lunge of the left shoulder, elbow, and wrist. Your head should come forward also, above your left foot. Imagine yourself to be aiming at a ball, and see that your left wrist is in a line between your eyes and some object, say a chair's leg in the bedroom. (ii.) Jerk the forearm (and wrist) as if you were whipping a peg-top or shaking out a clogged stylographic pen.

For the wrist and fingers. Flex and twist the wrist and each finger far and fast in various directions. After freedom and pace have been acquired, but not before, some strength can be added by resistance--as by holding a dumb-bell during the movements, or by using some grip machine.

Let us apply these--a few out of many mechanisms for all-round batting--to forward-play. The excellent words of Mr. Edward Lyttelton must be quoted first. He says:--

"You will see from these directions that it is a very complex action, far from easy to do all at once, so that by careful practice if not by the light of nature you must first learn to do it properly without the ball, then with it. Establish the motion as a habit before the stress of the crisis begins.... It is thought that just as great players of yore reached eminence without being subject to coaching in early youth, or indeed in some cases after being completely self-taught, so boys of the present day would stand a better chance if they were less drilled than they sometimes are, and were left to find the use of their limbs by a vigorous, if unkempt style of hitting. The Englishman's instinct, said a Frenchman, is to go out of doors and hit or kick something as hard as he can. This being so, why not let boys learn to hit as they please till they are sixteen or seventeen, and then perhaps a few rules might be taught them? But if taught beforehand, they only cramp the style, and take away the enjoyment of the game. Nature must be the best teacher; etc., etc.... But it is not at all easy to secure this habit, and therefore you should remember it carefully in your bedroom...."

Pretend that you are going to play forward, and hold a stick in your hands. Now, moving your fingers as you come forward (see below), lunge with your left foot along a straight line, and send your head over your left foot. (If you tend to deviate from the line, probably towards the left, then exaggerate towards the right.) Keep your eye on the foot till the foot can take care of itself. Regard it as a servant that you must first watch carefully till the correct work shall have become half-automatic; then only an occasional glance of supervision will be required. Add to this lunge the extended lunge of the left wrist, elbow, and shoulder straight along a line parallel to and slightly to the right of the left foot.

The stick should be lifted straight back and up before the stroke (though the blade of a bat, as in Racquets, will face outwards at the top of the lift), and should then come forward in a direct line close to the left foot, and afterwards follow through beyond the left foot. Do not forget to keep both that foot along *its* line and the left wrist along *its* line by aiming say at some spot on the wall. After the lunge with the whole weight, recover balance, look up, and prepare to run forward. Later on, do this and actually start forwards a few steps. That is part of the physical apparatus which a good average forward-stroke demands. There is no space to describe the requirements of the other strokes--the cut, etc. They can easily be seen from the photographs and from the play of experts. And some additional exercises will be offered under the special headings below.

PRACTICE OUTSIDE THE NETS.

In addition to these and other movements, which may be tried at first either before a large mirror or else with a teacher behind to correct and perform correctly by way of instruction, Mr. Edward Lyttelton mentions the practice of certain strokes with a ball in the pavilion. Any old room will do. And the narrower the implement of batting the more easily it will show the errors of batting; the lighter the implement, the better it will develop pace and freedom. A stump or stick or broomstick will do; a light indiarubber ball will do.

If you cannot get a bowler, then you can throw the ball--a Lawn Tennis ball will do--up against a wall, and play forward or back to it with a stick. I know a player who did this with very good results.

Games of "Snob-cricket," and of Cricket with smaller ball and narrower bat, should be far more frequently tried for the sake of practice.

Imaginary strokes may be made during idle moments. Fancy yourself playing straight forward with full weight, or fancy yourself stepping across and back with the right foot and then cutting with a jerk of shoulder and forearm and some wrist-flick. I do a great deal of Racquet and Tennis practice in this way; needless to say, I play infinitely better in imagination than in reality! But I know that thus I help to make my ideal real. After such an imagination-practice I often reproduce improved strokes with a light racket-handle in my bedroom.

NET-PRACTICE.

If too many bowlers are bowling at one net, the variety is bad; in actual play one has no such variety in a single over. I would rather see three bowlers each bowl an over in turn, while the two others field. If you cannot reform this, then make the best of it by trying to remember the previous balls of each bowler, as if you were playing several games of chess at the same time.

Begin on good wickets, so as to habituate confidence and pluck. Don't practise correct Cricket (you can, however, practise the bold running-out game for a caking wicket) if the ground be fiery. Loss of nerve is fatal.

Play safely and gently till you get set; defend against the difficult balls; then, when you are set, meet and hit every ball, except for the rare "half-cock" strokes to which you may have to resort.

The next stage is to place the ball. While on the one hand you must count every chance you give, and every ball an inch or two from the bails, as a wicket down, you may, on the other hand, venture on experiments; you may determine to hit a ball pitched too short or too far up to one of two or three places.

Notice the sort of ball which beats you most frequently, and find out why it does so, and how you can best play it--perhaps this may be by stepping back or forwards and turning it into some other ball.

Aim at developing your individual strong points, *but*--

(1.) Do not do this until you have mastered the fundamental elements of various strokes; and

(2.) Do not be content with this. Gradually bring up your weak points to the level of your strong points. Indeed, practise them far more than your strong points.

GAMES.

While many hints must be reserved for the last section of this chapter, we may here say a few words about games as distinct from training, exercises, and net-practice; though it will be necessary to touch on the importance of training, for success in the games. What better help is there against the nervousness so fatal to success than the habit of full and deep breathing? Can you be nervous at all so long as you breathe fully and deeply? What better help, towards the steadiness and confidence so important to success, than the clear eye that comes from clean living, the feeling that the fingers "nip" the bat, the feeling that the correct mechanisms are under control, the self-reliance gained by net-practice on good pitches?

This steadiness is most necessary at the beginning of an innings. As we mentioned above, two of the great players tell us that at first they were content to defend, often merely to stop balls without attacking them. Historians and natural historians and other scientists show us that each individual human being in itself reproduces quickly the past evolutions of the human race, being, for example, a seed, fish-like, reptile-like, ape-like, then man-like. So each individual innings may quickly reproduce the past stages of practice and progress, safety and defence coming before severity and attack, except where--as on some caking wickets--safety and defence consist in an apparently rash rushing out to smite. As a rule, however, no liberties should be taken until the bowling has been mastered and the eye is "in." Time may be saved if one watches the previous batsmen and finds out how they get out. Moreover, just as Spofforth first tested the pitch and its pace and peculiarities on any given day, before he bowled his best, so a batsman may also test the pitch.

For different pitches demand different plays--different mechanisms, different tactics. Few, like Shrewsbury, have a style adapted alike to the billiard-table ground and the drying-ground. Ranjitsinhji's book gives most useful remarks on these differences.

While you are batting, count a chance as a blessed indication of error; treat it as I treat a premonitory pain--do not wait for the illness itself, but find out and correct the mistake at once. You may have to exaggerate in the opposite direction--perhaps to play forward further out to the right than seems natural to you on that day.

WAITING FOR THE BALL.

Guard is taken not only to give one a sense of the direction of any ball, but also to give one the correct place for the right foot: the toe of the right foot should be quite near to the block. Therefore one should not have a block either to the off (in which case the right toes might be in front of the wicket), or short and too near the wicket.

Before and after taking guard one should look round to see how the field is placed.

As to the waiting-position, one may try several and choose that which is the best basis and starting-pose for *most* ordinary strokes. But first one should develop the various muscles, especially those needed for the quick movements; otherwise one might adopt an attitude suited for safe play when a more Jessop-like or at least a more Stoddart-like or Abel-like attitude might be better for one. A good attitude for many will be Shrewsbury's as seen in the Photograph (I.). The body should be nearly sideways,

I.--Waiting for the ball, with the weight balanced almost evenly upon the two feet (which are near together), but rather on the right foot.

[*To face page 22.*

with the legs (or only the left leg) very slightly bent, and ready to move backwards or forwards. One should not be stiff, but should be inclined to looseness, until one knows which ball is coming; till then one should be ready to run or jump out if it should be desirable. The feet should probably be quite near to one another, the right being near the crease and parallel to the wicket, the left outside the crease and pointing more towards the bowler. Probably both should be resting on their balls, and rather--so Mr. Fry advises--on the insides of their balls.

The weight of most batsmen should be upon the right foot, the batsman's basis. Abel stands on the ball of his right foot; that is good if one be quick-footed. Ranjitsinhji explains some of the reasons why the weight should rest on the right foot--he instances several forms of exercise, such as boxing; for Tennis and Racquets I have spent hours in practising quick movements in all directions with the stiff right leg as my pivot. The left foot may be slightly up and prepared to move out along some forward line. In case of a late cut one has time to shift the weight on to it and make *it* the pivot.

The bat is usually held with one hand near the top of the handle and the other hand near the middle of the handle; if one holds the right hand lower down one gets more control, but may lose some pace; one is more apt to stoop, and to lift the ball. But for some strokes, as for certain late cuts, the shifted grip is often preferable; one should be able to slip the right hand down the handle towards the blade, near to which so many of the stone-wallers love to keep it. As the right foot and leg hold the ground more firmly, so does the right hand and wrist hold the bat more firmly, though there should be no tight and tense grip till the stroke is being made. One can--as Abel and Shrewsbury put it--"feel the nip" of the bat without any unnecessary tension. Not a few players have the grip of the two hands almost equal.

The left elbow should be well up, so as to keep the handle of the bat nearer to the bowler and thus to prevent a chance of catches. And the whole body and head should be well up as the bowler begins to bowl, so that the best possible view may be given.

One must watch the fingers and wrist and arm of the bowler; a change in his fingers

II.--Forward play: the bat has been drawn straight up and back (not in a curve) before the stroke.

[*To face page 25.*

will mean a change of the ball he will bowl. Thus Hirst's balls will differ according to the way in which his fingers are arranged (see the photographs). Abel generally watches the wrist rather than the fingers.

While the bowler is bowling, one should usually draw the bat up and back, without flourish, in the line opposite to the line of the approaching ball. The photograph of Shrewsbury (II.) shows the bat lifted for a straight ball which he is going to play (not drive) straight forward. By lifting the bat one gets more impetus and can use one's height and weight better.

Attention and alertness--these are to be maintained. "This one thing I do now," "On this depends everything"; such are samples of the suggestions which I often make to myself at my own games. Yet I try to economise energy and not to waste any of it; attention without tension, alertness without fidgetiness--these are right.

BACK-PLAY; THE GLIDE; THE HALF-COCK.

"Timing the ball is the secret," says Giffen. It is *a* secret, not *the* secret. Nor is it a simple rule; timing is (see page 7) a concoction of many good things.

A simpler general rule is not to leave a large space between the bat and the legs, lest one should be bowled off one's pads. The photograph of Abel shows no intervening space at all.

Another simple general (but not universal) rule is to end up--as in forward play--with the handle held by the *first finger and thumb of the right hand and of the left;* the other three fingers scarcely have any influence here. The nails of all four fingers--as in the photograph--should face the bowler (or yourself if you were opposite a mirror). The bat must not be tilted upwards nor drawn back behind the line of the right foot, which is firmly on the ground, and is certainly not drawn away to the leg-side.

About the "fixed right foot" there is--as we shall see--a great fallacy; theory has been allowed to controvert the practice of the leading experts. Shrewsbury in the photograh (III.) has his right foot firm indeed, and not shifted to the leg-side, but back almost to the wicket itself. W. G., in a photograph in Ranjitsinhji's book, has his right foot back, though not nearly so far back. I scarcely ever see a player whose regular *habit* is not to shift back his right foot somewhat

III.--Playing back: the right foot has retired nearer the wicket, so as to give longer time for seeing the ball.

NOTE.--The bat should be held straight. This photograph was taken before Shrewsbury was in practice.

[*To face page 26.*

in back play. Shrewsbury will tell one to get back far enough, moving back with the ball. This obviously gives one more time to see the ball and its break, turning a ball that is just a trifle short into a ball that is nearly a long hop; if the legs be--as they often are--in front of the wicket, so as to give a still better sight of the ball and also to save a play-on, then the retreat of the right foot is obviously useful. Others, however, do not move it in front of the wicket. But nearly all back-play is actually practised with the retirement of the right foot. Murdoch's words are worth quoting at some length:--

"In the majority of cases, my experience has been that, by moving the right foot as much or as little as judgment dictates, the stroke is made with far more ease than by having your right foot a fixture. If you will take the trouble to notice all players, you will see for yourself that in almost every case when they are playing back the right foot is always moved. And, again, you will find you have far more command and power over the ball, and especially so over a rising one, and you can finish your stroke in a far safer way.... My advice to you is to move the right foot when, in your judgment, it requires it; if you find you can play the ball with ease by not moving it, well and good; but should you at any time think you could play the ball better by getting back a little, why do so, and you will find it will give you a particle more time and enable you to make things very much easier.

"I think the art of boxing very applicable to forward and back play of cricket, for whilst boxing is nearly all forward strokes, there are many times when a boxer has to get back, and he generally finds what a great difference there is in receiving a hit whilst standing principally on his right foot, and when he has moved it a few inches in getting back. So it is with your back-play at cricket, the velocity of the ball is not so great two feet back from your crease as it is right on it. The advantage of time is no doubt momentary, but still it is an advantage, and one that I have proved and seen to be very beneficial."

One kind of glide-stroke forms a special branch of back-play: it is to be seen in the photograph of Abel (IV.). Ranjitsinhji is the master of this most useful stroke; he plays it for balls on the wicket as well as for balls to *leg*. Others use it chiefly or solely for balls off the wicket. For this stroke I believe every player has the right foot back. The bat's face is held not flat towards the bowler, but slanting in one of many directions on the leg-side, according to the spot to which one wishes to place the ball.

The "half-cock" stroke is Grace's favourite help in time of trouble. When he hesitates between forward and back-play, and especially after he has decided on forward-play and

IV.--The glide: both feet well back.

[*To face page 28.*

* * * * *

V.--Playing back: right foot retired, to give extra time for seeing the ball; weight on right foot. This is Shrewsbury's stroke when he feels "beaten" by the bowler.

[*To face page 29.*

then doubts whether he can reach out near enough to the pitch of the ball to smother the ball, he is content to strike the ball scarcely at all, if at all, and to hold his bat half way between its forward and back positions, and wait in hope.

Shrewsbury, however, if the ball be straight, prefers to bring his bat straight down on to the block. He is to be seen doing this in the photograph (V.).

It appears to me that, as most Lawn Tennis players learn back-play securely before they learn forward-play (play, i.e., at the net), so most cricketers should learn back-play securely; they should learn to play forward, of course; but, as Mr. C. B. Fry says, they should not learn that only. Inasmuch as back-play is the easier and more natural--except for the art of not drawing away the right foot towards the leg side--it should probably precede the mastery of forward-play, towards which mastery the "half-cock" stroke might form a transition step.

FORWARD-PLAY AND SAFE DRIVING.

There may be days when scarcely any forward-play is needed; there may be experts who prefer back-play even on fast and true pitches, just as Mr. A. W. Gore, the amateur Lawn Tennis champion of 1901, prefers habitual back-play at his game. But every player should be able to play forward, particularly to swift good-length balls on quick plumb-wickets which are either too dry or else too slippery to bite the ball and allow it to break; on the fast slippery wickets, however, forward-play must be accurate, because of the occasional shooter. Besides the safety of such forward-play, since it can smother the ball, there is the extra delight of meeting if not of attacking, and also of performing a movement which is not by any means natural--the extra delight of overcoming a mechanical difficulty.

We may begin to study this forward-play (for which we have already offered certain exercises--see above) by a couple of quotations from well-known writers.

"The golden rules to guide the beginner in playing forward may be very briefly stated. (1.) Play forward when the ball is fairly well pitched up, but remember that the faster the bowling and the faster the wicket the more frequently will forward-play be the safer style of play. (2.) Keep the bat quite

* * * * *

VI.--Playing forward to a ball on the off: the straight bat has passed near and beyond the left foot in a "follow-through." Notice the fingers, especially the first finger and thumb of the left hand. At the end of the stretch the left arm is fully extended, and the right heel has come off the ground.

[*Between pages 30 and 31.*

* * * * *

VII.--Playing forward to a ball slightly to the leg side: see remark on previous photograph, and notice the head well over the bat-handle.

[*Between pages 30 and 31.*

VIII.--Playing forward to a straight ball: see remarks on previous photographs.

[*Between pages 30 and 31.*

straight and the left shoulder and elbow well forward. (3.) Get as near to the pitch of the ball as possible. (4.) Do not put the bat further forward than the level of the left foot, which ought to be thrown right forward."

"No forward-stroke is absolutely safe unless the ball is smothered. There are many very beautiful strokes effected by forward-play at the rising ball. Such strokes, however, are purely plumb-wicket strokes."

In the face of this latter quotation, and of (3) of the first quotation, and in the face of the habitual practice of many leading experts (see Photographs VI., VII., VIII., of Abel and Shrewsbury) in following through with the bat beyond the left foot, the statement in (4) is absurd. And yet, as we shall see in the Chapter on Fallacies, it appears in almost every work on Cricket.

Personally I should far sooner see the general rule stated as follows:--

"At the root of good ordinary forward-play lies *extension* both direct (not curved) and well-timed and well-co-ordinated (not too early or too late, and not piece by piece--for example, first the foot, then the left elbow), and fast and powerful (not slow and tame), and full (not arrested); at the root of it lies such extension of right leg, left foot, left shoulder, left elbow, left wrist; *but within the limits of power, and of balance or rapid recovery of balance.*" When Abel or Shrewsbury can thus safely and strongly reach out an extra fifteen inches beyond the left foot, and thus smother a ball and its break, why forbid it? If only in case a ball hangs a bit, and also for the sake of the follow-through--I believe that nearly every ball-game stroke demands a follow-through--such a passing of the blade's end beyond the left foot may be advisable.

Be this as it may--and it must be settled by practice, not by theory--at any rate the law holds good that for ordinary ground-play (as distinct from the drive out of the ground) the left wrist must come before the right, the right shoulder being kept down.

The base, the safe aphorme of forward-play, is the firm right foot (nearly parallel to the three wickets) and the straight right l*eg*. From this base the left leg has, as it were, to radiate forward in one or another straight line towards the approaching balls; not straight at those balls, but a few inches to one's left; certainly not necessarily straight forward down the line from wicket to wicket, as the forward play of Abel to a ball on the off will show (see Photograph VI.); in fact, to a left hand bowler round the wicket one should as a rule *not* play along this line, but along a line further outwards to one's right. The left toe points, and the left foot moves, not *at* but towards the line of the approaching ball, allowance being made for a curl or a break that will alter this line. It is the line that the ball will be making just when it strikes the bat (or, rather, just when it is struck by the bat) that has to be met by the bat, which must move in a line a few inches to the right of the left foot. The line both of left foot and of bat must be direct, not curved.

Over one's bat comes one's head: as Abel says, one must get above the ball and smell it. The bat itself, for ground-play, must not be tilted with its blade nearer to the bowler than its handle is, lest a catch be sent up. Its direction from the line when one lifts it before the stroke (see Photograph II.), right up to the end of the follow-through (see Photograph VIII.), must be as straight as possible; like a boxer's blow straight from the shoulder, and not like the swirling arm of the unskilled navvy, even if both these movements might reach the same goal eventually. The curved line means a loss of time and of power, as well as a risk--for it allows a smaller margin of error.

The stroke should be all in one piece, the power beginning when the bat is near to the left leg, and of course reaching its fulness from each part of the mechanism just when the blade hits the ball.

To what part of the mechanism would one do best to attend? The firm right foot is the base, the *point d'appui*, the *terminus a quo*. I should say that the *terminus ad quem*, the point of limit, should be the outside joint of the left wrist. Let that go right out to its stretch. Most of us, by taking thought, *can* add an inch or so to our reach. I added two inches to my (easy) forward reach within two months.

The hand's grip should change as the left wrist shoots outward. In the waiting position the bowler (or you yourself in a mirror) can see the back of your left hand; then

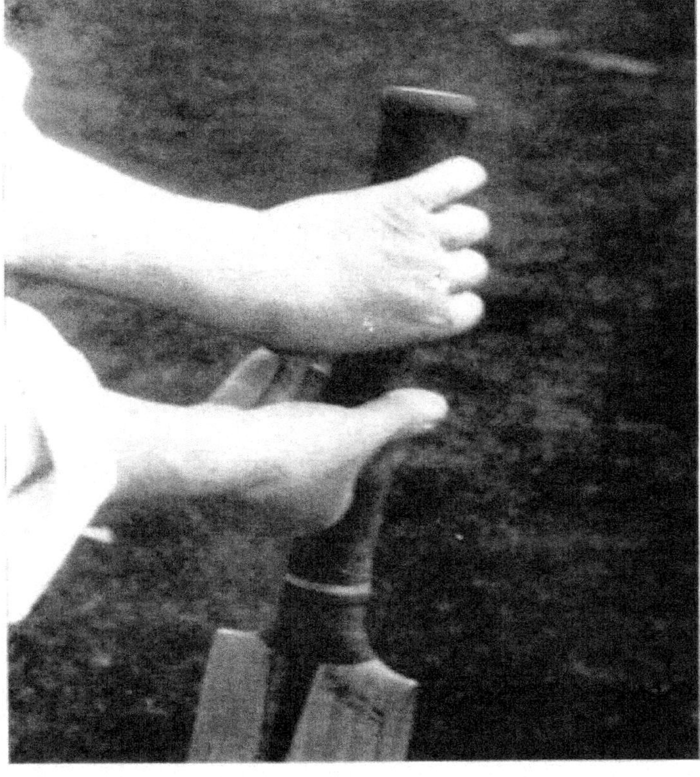

* * * * *

IX.--Position of hands and fingers at the end of the forward stroke: the left hand has shifted round, the right hand holds the bat with thumb and first finger only.

[*To face page 35.*

back and up goes the bat--not too far, but enough to get power (my own ordinary Tennis and Racquet strokes and many a golfer's ordinary strokes go up and back quite a short way as compared with the old-fashioned "complete" swing); then, as the bat comes down and forward, you yourself (if you had not your eye on the ball) should be able to see the back of your bat and above it the back of your left hand (as in Photograph IX. of Shrewsbury's hands). So far as the left side is concerned, the stroke is an exaggeration of a left-handed backhand stroke, except that the thumb in cricket does not support the handle as it often does in Racquets.

If any one cannot yet play forward, but wishes to learn the art, let him practise (as I have recently done) this turn of the fingers, this outward stretch of left wrist, left elbow, left shoulder, straight along a line, full, swift, weighty. It is amazing how soon the straight line can become easy if one works faithfully along a line upon the floor and opposite a mirror, correcting all errors by the opposite exaggerations, but first of all securing the foundation--the long straight lunge of the left foot. Sandow and all high authorities say, Throw the whole will, focus the whole attention, concentrate the whole mind, fix the whole vital force, upon the muscles which you are using; first do this upon the left foot, then upon the left wrist (if not upon the handle of the bat, strange as it may sound).

Having acquired this free forward line, then practise a speedy recovery of balance afterwards, and a readiness to start running. Later on, add to these two a few actual steps. Eventually, though you may have had to conquer each mechanism by itself, as I conquered every part of my Tennis and Racquet strokes separately, yet you will be able to combine them together so harmoniously that no one will guess or believe how you gained your stroke. It appears so exactly like a unity, so exactly like one single action--that lunge with full weight, and recovery of equilibrium--that people tell me I never could have learnt it part-by-part. But I *did*. I can tell every part, though now the whole move is a unit. There is absolutely no necessity to begin by doing the whole stroke at once, so long as eventually you can combine the various members of it into a harmonious whole. Otherwise any one individual bad part may spoil the whole effect.

This correct stroke frustrates the bowler's attempt to make you tilt up your bat's blade and send a catch: having your left wrist well forward beyond your right, you keep your strokes down. Another common fault besides the tilted bat is the crooked bat, the bat of which the blade is too far to the off; this fault is obviated chiefly by the straight right leg: bend the right leg, and the tendency is for both these faults to appear.

Forward play may be either defensive or offensive. The latter kind merges into the ground-drive. In either case the average-eyed person must get to the pitch of the ball and smother it, or must not play forward, but either do the half-cock stroke or else step back and give himself the largest possible time in which to see the ball's flight. The defensive should as a rule precede the offensive, both while one is learning to play forward and also while one is beginning any innings at a net or in a game. A few forward stretches before play will perhaps save a premature dismissal through stiffness.

In forward ground-driving the rule of not letting the bat's blade go beyond the left foot is far more reasonable. One must get well over the ball, the power coming chiefly from just that jerk of shoulder, fore-arm, and wrist which Latham and Pettitt and a few others use at Racquets--the jerk of some whippers of peg-tops. But for this drive the bat need not move *quite* so near to the left foot. Moreover the bat may finish up with a smaller follow-through. Let the forward left elbow arrest the swing of the right arm, lest the bat be tilted and the ball rise: that wrench of the left elbow-joint is a satisfactory sign.

The forward off-drive (for a ball not coming at the wicket) allows of a far freer swing, and, if you see it well, of a far less straight bat. It needs more right wrist and less left elbow restraint. Indeed, it may end up with the bat over the left shoulder. Photograph XIII. shows Abel's position for such a drive, though the position is better suited for a cut-drive.

For the forward on-drive the left foot is pointed out towards mid-on.

THE PULL AND HIGH DRIVE.

There used to be a fallacy that the pull was bad form because it was ungraceful; but now-a-days grace is of little account

X.--Preparing to drive with a pull: the left leg is well out so that the bat may get nearer to the pitch of the ball.

unless it is useful. Hirst's pull will count as four, while graceful "good form" will courteously return the same ball to the bowler and score nothing. It was W. G. and his brother who subordinated so-called art to utilitarianism. The only valid objection to the pull is that it is most dangerous as a habitual stroke; whereas for a full pitch or a long hop it may be, as Shrewsbury says, least dangerous as well as most paying, since it may need less power and may go to a part of the ground least thickly studded with fielders.

The mistake is not in the pulling *per se*, but, as Ranjitsinhji insists, in the choice of the wrong ball for pulling, or else--we may add--in the wrong way of pulling the right ball.

As there is elsewhere a forward-play as well as a back-play, so there is with pulls. Abel is shown giving a forward pull, in Photograph X.; notice that the left foot is right out so that the bat gets well to the pitch of the ball. If one could always ensure that, pulling would be the best stroke in the game. This step out adds to the safety of the pull when the ball will pitch say two yards from the batsman.

The back-play pull is for a shorter ball. Hirst is making such a pull in Photograph XI. (and Photograph XII. which represents a different kind of pull by Shrewsbury). Hirst has moved back and turned a somewhat short ball into a long hop. Into this stroke he will put the full body-swing from the hips. He might do this stroke equally well with a good full pitch to the off. To run out (either to slow bowling or to ordinary bowling on a difficult wicket) and then to "volley" round to leg used to be the one stroke that I could do reasonably well. Even then I often erred in running out timidly and in using my wrists rather than my trunk and shoulders.

Whereas the long hop and the ordinary full pitch may be placed thus, the half-volley can seldom be safely pulled. It is hard to direct. But with all these strokes, whether pulls or drives, the law of "the left elbow and wrist well forward to prevent catches" may be ignored if one can get to the pitch of the ball by coming forward, or else get it as a long hop by stepping back, and then can place it safely away from any fielder. If one can, then one need never mind about sending

XI.--Preparing to pull a short ball: right foot across, so as to help the stroke well round to leg.

[*Between pages 40 and 41.*

XII.--Preparing to pull a short ball: right foot across and well back so as to make the short ball still shorter.

[*Between pages 40 and 41.*

XIII.--Hook-stroke to leg: both feet well back, but weight on right foot.

[*Between pages 40 and 41.*

XIV.--Cut-drive. Right leg firm and straight, left leg bent and well across.

[*To face page 41.*

high balls or playing with a crooked bat.

The useful hook-stroke to leg is seen in Photograph XIII.

CUTTING.

Ranjitsinhji rightly distinguishes several kinds of cuts, and advanced players must be referred to his book for details. Here one must be content to notice the cut-drive (forward-play to some spot between point and extra-cover, as in Photograph XIV. of Abel), and the late-cut (back-play to some spot between point and short slip, as in the photographs of Abel and Shrewsbury). Here once more we have forward and back play, the latter allowing more time.

The cut-drive is good for a short ball on the off. The left foot is sent out to the off, the bat swings back and generally somewhat up, very much as it does to the pull-drive. Abel is seen preparing for a cut-drive in Photograph XIV. He will get right on to the top of the ball.

The downward movement, for the sake of safety, applies also to the late-cut, with regard to which we have already exposed the fallacy that it is a stroke done entirely with the wrists.[4] The wrists may do some of the directing at the last moment, but the large movement and the force is *usually* given chiefly by the fore-arm-jerk, the shoulder-jerk, a little trunk-movement, and (with some players) the step with the right foot across the wicket. Let a hundred experts make imaginary or real late-cuts for half-an-hour, and I guarantee that the wrists will not be the only parts that ache. Indeed I have seen many players cut safely and effectively with absolutely rigid wrists. As I have already said, the motion is nearer to that of shaking out a stylographic pen or whipping a peg-top; it is akin to the Racquet stroke of Latham or the Tennis stroke of Pettitt. Watch the forearm and the shoulder of a stripped player, and this will be clear.

The late-cut is most safely used against fast and not too short bowling on a quick pitch; it does not oppose the ball's flight, but rather increases or at least directs that flight. It is not to be rashly tried

XV.--The late cut: right foot well across, left leg extended so far as to bring heel off ground.

[*Between pages 42 and 43.*

XVI.--The late cut: right foot well across, left leg extended.

[*Between pages 42 and 43.*

against slow bowling, especially if this breaks much, on a slow or caking wicket; for it needs very accurate timing.

In this late-cut the right leg is moved back and across the wicket (see Photograph XIV. of Shrewsbury's legs), so that the left leg and foot now does what the right leg and foot do for the other strokes--namely, serve as a pivot. Some move the right foot and then make the stroke; I believe Ranjitsinhji generally prefers this plan. Others, like Abel, often make the stroke as a single movement. Others use now one plan and now the other. Anyhow the weight passes from the left on to the right leg, which is bent. Shrewsbury, in the photograh (XV.), is allowing his left foot to rise slightly on its ball. Contrast Abel, in XVI.

He does not alter his ordinary grip, and he uses his wrists a good deal; others let their right hand slide down the handle towards the blade, and sometimes let their left hand slide after it. The bat strikes downwards, passing about twelve inches over the wicket.

The direction of the cut is most important: this depends partly on the presence or absence of a wrist movement, partly, as Ranjitsinhji says, on the moment at which one strikes the ball--the earlier hit goes squarer (nearer to point), the later hit goes finer (nearer to short slip).

The late-cut involves not a little risk. It may be well at the beginning of an innings to study the art of

LEAVING BALLS ALONE.

A good length or "blind" ball on the off-side, and a certain kind of bumping long hop (almost out of one's reach) are intended for a catch behind the wicket. Some may be cut or driven, but it would be safer to let a few pass by (unless they are going to break in) till one sees what they are doing. The continued practice of this plan is not for the good of Cricket as a form of sport.

The use of the legs to defend the wicket has been another much-discussed topic. Ranjitsinhji rightly points out that it requires skill and is not unknown in the play of the best experts. Here as elsewhere the fault lies less in the use than in the excessive use.

MOVING OUT.

If Shrewsbury and others have been censured as too cautious in letting certain balls alone, and in playing certain other balls with their pads instead of their bats, the runner-out is censured for the opposite reason--for a ridiculous rashness. This is a fallacy. To run out is often the safest policy: it may mean to smother an otherwise difficult ball. Abel and Jessop, like Latham at Racquets and Tennis, play with their feet as much as with their heads. The best illustration that occurs to me of "the wisdom of anticipation" (stigmatized as "the folly of rashness") is the running up to volley or half-volley the service at Racquets. Often one can take a ball best by letting it nearly fall to the ground at its second bounce--that is, by turning into a "long hop"; but if it be a good length service, or one with a heavy cut, it may be more prudent to run up and thus change it into a comparatively harmless plaything, as a child may deal with a snake by fearless handling. Murdoch is most emphatic on this point, when he says:--"No, I think the feet play very important parts in batting, and both of them should have the greatest scope possible. I advise all players to learn to use their feet quickly and well, and it will be the means of getting you out of many a difficulty. By being able to get to a ball quickly you make it an easy one where if you had remained in your crease you would have found it a most difficult one to stop. Once you get into the way of doing this you will never move the right foot unless you require to do so to make your stroke. In all forward play it is absolutely necessary for you to keep the right foot well on the ground."

There are three ways of moving out to a ball; in all three ways one must not draw the right foot away, but one must keep the right foot as the pivot; and one must come out wholeheartedly, not hesitatingly.

Shrewsbury will often jump out, coming down on to his right foot first with his body-weight upon its ball. He who tries this should be prepared to keep his balance and if necessary to jump back again into his ground.

Most others run out sideways with small or large steps. See Photograph XVII.

Abel runs out more quickly than these. His legs, as it were, intertwine neatly in the way shown in Photograph XVIII. His first step, with the left foot, is well across the

XVII.--The way of running out with fairly long steps, weight should be chiefly on right foot, and right leg should be ready to serve as firm pivot.

[*Between pages 46 and 47.*

XVIII.--Abel's way of running out, with feet interlacing.

[*Between pages 46 and 47.*

wicket and towards the off-side; his second step, with the right foot; the action may be repeated.

This sideways running is not easy: it needs considerable practice backwards and forwards before one can not only do it but also maintain one's poise and be ready to hit the ball afterwards. A jump or a run out, even with a loss of poise, may be far better policy than to wait for a "teaser." Two quotations from high authority are worth citing here.

"I do not think that batsmen run out enough at slow bowling or at lobs. For some undiscovered reason, there is a floating idea that running out and rashness are synonymous. As a matter of fact, to run out is often the safest thing one can do. It makes a difficult ball into an easy one, and often enables the batsman to make a forcing-stroke along the ground instead of a risky high-drive. The man who plays cautiously is invariably regarded with reverence and favour by those who know. He is supposed to play the correct game. He often ties himself into extraordinary knots by playing what he considers a safe dashing game. There are some players who, not being quick on their feet, ought never to run out."

"A running-out stroke should be played with the same amount of care and concentration as a back-stroke. There is an air of abandon about quick-footed players which is very deceptive; they often run out to meet the ball, because they feel safer in doing so than in staying at home."

Short balls or balls well off the wicket are seldom to be met in this way unless one is a Jessop. But whatever ball be anticipated in this way let it be sought with full pace and intent to "volley". If one must be stumped, then, as Grace and others say, one may just as well be many yards out of one's ground as be only one yard of it.

RUNNING.

An obvious advantage in moving out is that, if your partner is backing up, you have every chance of making a safe run.

Quick starting and quick moving between the wickets are little cultivated. Yet a game of tip-and-run will show how many runs can be stolen. Too little account is taken of the pace at which the ball has been hit, the place to which it has been hit, the individual to whom it has been hit, the side of that individual, left or right, to which it has been hit, and so on.

The general rule is that the player in whose sight the struck ball appears most clearly (namely, the batsman for balls in front of him, his partner for balls behind him) shall call at once and call loudly. The non-caller shall either trust and obey, or else immediately call a loud "No."

Both players should start at once from their right toes, and should run the first run as briskly as if a second were sure to follow. Giffen laments the small care paid to this art. He says:--

"One most important point connected with batting is running between the wickets. Really it is almost heartrending to see the immense number of runs, to say nothing of the wickets, which are lost through bad judgment. A batsman wants to study the pace at which a ball is travelling."

The non-batsman should back up well; a few yards may be gained in this way, and also by the habit of running the bat along the ground just inside the crease.

A useful position for turning at the crease is to be seen in Photograph XIX., of Shrewsbury. By the rapid change while the bat is held at full stretch one may gain an appreciable amount of time and space.

GENERAL HINTS.

The first pieces of advice to all players of games will be, "Get at the reason why, and the means by which." Why should one not flourish the bat before a stroke? Partly because this sends the bat out of the straight line and loses time. Why should one move the bat near to the left foot in forward-play? Partly because this will give power by keeping the weight of the body near to the bat, and because it will give safety, by allowing no space for the ball to pass between bat and *leg*. Merely to say to a beginner "Don't be afraid of the ball" may not be enough; he should know that, if he draws his right foot towards the leg-side, he will lose his pivot and will tend not to play the ball down and not to meet it along its line of approach. If he bends his right leg, the same result

XIX.--Turning quickly at the crease after the first run.

[*To face page 50.*

may follow. How can he keep the ball down and meet it along its line of approach? By attending to his left foot in practice, or by getting some one to watch his practice or play from behind.

Having found out and mastered the muscular mechanisms as well as the *raisons d'etre* for each of them, let the learner be prepared to try new things and to judge them by their results. In January, 1902, in my thirty-fourth year, I changed my Racquet and Tennis stroke from a full swing to a more "partial" jerk. In case it did not suit me, I was prepared to go back to the old. As a matter of fact, the new did suit me.

In this case I imitated Latham and (to some extent) Pettitt. They were of about my own height. I did not imitate slavishly or in trust, but in hope and because I saw good sense in what they did. In Cricket many might hold that even slavish imitation is better than rank failure.

To take an example. Few batsmen play well on difficult wickets. Shrewsbury does. I would sooner imitate his style and methods on difficult wickets than go on failing to score. There is no particular reason why his style and methods should *not* turn out to be mine as well. I cannot tell till I have experimented.

The batsman, as Mr. C. B. Fry says, should be able to play all games and strokes--forward, back, cut, and, let us add, tip and run. He must be able to keep his wicket up, to stop good balls (as Shrewsbury advises) and then punish bad balls; but he must also be able to force the game, especially if the bowling be too hard to enable him to stay in long.

Especially should he be "nippy on his feet"--Abel's rule. He need not use them always, but he must be ready to use them. So with the pull: he must not be tied down by a law "Thou shalt not pull." A short ball can often be pulled quite safely: it need not always be hit to mid-off. Scarcely any rule is absolute. We hear that the right leg should not be bent. Good. But when we see Grace hitting effectively to the on with a decidedly bent right leg, we suspect that there may be times when this is useful. It is only as *general* rules for most people that maxims are to be laid down. "Stand upright" says the theorist; he even quotes successful examples. But the individual may be nearer to Stoddart or Jessop than to Palairet. Let the individual try both ways, if not in games, then at the nets.

Reserve some force, says Mr. R. Lyttelton in the Badminton Volume; Ranjitsinhji agrees--since the use of the full force may "give one away" and lose the balance. But Shrewsbury says, "Use the full force; a mis-hit then has more chance of going over the head of cover or some other fielder." Keep the ball down--that is a good enough rule; but if you can hit the ball safely away from or over the head of a fielder, why not? Again, we hear that the batsman should not stand with any part of his body in front of his wicket; yet many find it useful to do so, especially in case they snick the ball and might otherwise play on. Another hint that may not always be helpful is "not to make up your mind what you will do until the bowler's intention has shown itself; for, if you decide, he will alter his intention." This presupposes that the bowler is observant and intelligent, whereas ordinary bowlers are not. In Racquets, on the same principle, I have been told not to pledge myself to any set action before the server has served; that is sound sense so long as the server is likely to vary his service; whereas, if I *know* that he is going to pound away with the same sort of thing all the time, I should waste energy by perpetual alertness. I take for granted that the fool will serve foolishly, and I virtually settle my policy beforehand. It is not every bowler who demands alertness.

Of wider and more nearly universal application are such hints as "Face the left-hand bowler round the wicket differently from the bowler over the wicket; move your left foot out on different lines"; "Don't try risky attack till you are sure of safe defence, unless the wicket be extremely difficult"; "Don't attempt to place a half-volley very accurately"; "Watch and observe the ordinary curves and breaks of the ball according to this or that action"; "Notice how others as well as yourself are most apt to get out off certain balls--say off the breaking ball well-pitched up on the off"; "Practise wicket-keeping occasionally"; "Study each bowler's action before you go in"; "When you go in, be careful at first of touching balls on the off"; "Get the blind spots of the pitch in your mind's eye, so as to tell whether to play back or forward: the blind spot varies according to the pace of the ball, the state of the ground, etc."; "Get in your mind's eye a picture of the fielders; and, when you are set, place the easier balls between those fielders; but keep your real eye on the ball from the instant that it has left the bowler's hand"; "Find out your faults and practise the opposite faults." As Mr. Edward Lyttelton says, "If it appears that your strokes habitually fail to tell as they should, it will probably be owing to your body not being properly utilized, and a spell of bedroom practice should at once be inaugurated." You can even cultivate the opposite fault during the game itself. This is my habit during Tennis and Racquets matches: if I find myself playing too soon at the ball, I purposely try to play too late.

CHAPTER II.
BOWLING.

"Every cricketer should be able to bowl when called upon to do so by his captain. Every man who has played cricket has bowled at a net, and he certainly has an action which is different from everybody else's."--*From the Badminton Volume.*

"Anything that improves bowling even a little is to be looked upon as an unmixed boon to the game. The number of bowlers who have hitherto made an honest attempt to acquire the knack is extremely small, so that we need not forecast from the past what the future might be."--*Edward Lyttelton.*

INTRODUCTORY.

MORE bowlers and better bowlers are sadly needed if amateurs are to hold their own against professionals in other games besides Lawn Tennis and Ping-pong. Bowlers are more and more needed in these days of good pitches, when the caking ground, the bowler's conjuror, cannot be had to order.

The cause of the behindhandness of bowling is partly the excellence of the plumb-wicket, partly the rise of the Pro bowler (without a corresponding rise of the Pro or Amateur fielder), and partly the consequent head-play demanded of the bowler, who to-day must think hard and must also *be* hard--must endure. But the cause lies less in the degeneracy of the bowler than in the progress of the batsman and his chances of scoring, the use of the heavy roller (to which Mr. R. H. Lyttelton so often calls attention), and last but not least the fatal theory that the bowler is born not made.

Of course the bowler is born--who isn't? But whether or no he may be made if the right means be adopted, remains to be ascertained by experiment, the only teacher. We must suspend judgment, must insist on epokhe, until some sort of method of making a bowler has been fairly tried. We freely grant a certain "luck" in the finding of a natural action with free swing and fine break. Yet we may still believe that *proper* practice, as distinct from casual and persistent plugging, may work wonders.

Anyhow, all should learn to bowl a bit, not only for their own pleasure and in order to get a place in a team, but also because the future of Cricket largely depends on the excellence and the variety of the bowling.

More and superior bowlers are urgently wanted, whether wicket-keeping and fielding be improved or not (of course the worse the fielding is, the better the bowling must be); whether batting be cramped or not (see the Chapter on Reforms); and whether the conditions of bowling be improved or not, as by the smaller bat, the larger wicket, the shorter innings, the artificial pitch to take the full break, and so on.

There is a great opening for every one who can learn to bowl. Is there no *practical* advice to be offered besides such hints as: "Bowl naturally," "Have an easy swing," "Get the length," "Put on a break," "Use a high action," "Vary and conceal the pace, etc."? At present no writer says, "Develop the right muscles rightly first." No writer seems to have sought what muscles are used by most good bowlers, and how they may best be developed. As to the exercisers and developers, they are in my opinion excellent for mere increase in the size of certain muscles, for weight-lifting, for rowing, for gymnastics, for pushing in the football scrum, but infamously worse than useless for bowling purposes until speed has already been acquired. Later on, we shall expose a few fallacies about bowling, especially the fallacy that premature failure means perpetual disability, whereas the real fault may lie with the undeveloped mechanism of bowling; thus I myself after a few weeks of bedroom-practice had added an inch to the upward extension of my arm, and can move my wrist and fingers freely in more directions than before.

The first thing is to find out what muscles are used and how. This we may do by watching good bowlers like Hirst, and by asking them, at the beginning of the season, where they *ache*. These muscles we may practise by fast full movements and fast arrested movements, not by strain-exercises. Thus, when we find the first finger of the expert nearly worn out, we may conclude that this finger is a potent factor in success. Till we can use it, let us not despair. This is only one example. Personally I do not see how any one could expect to bowl decently with trunk, shoulder, wrist, and fingers as stiff as mine were.

Having found out the mechanisms, we must secure them; we must be content with nothing short of mastery, especially in these days of plumb-wickets. The beginning need not be too fast; medium bowlers have succeeded as well as fast, and have lasted longer.

And now as to the

ORDER OF LEARNING.

Bowling is in Cricket very much what serving is (or should be) in Racquets and Tennis; very much the same order can be observed as in these games, apart from the bowling at nets, at a stump, and against a wall--all of which are useful afterwards.

1. First comes *the mechanism*, the control of the requisite muscles and combinations of muscles. For this control certain exercises may be outlined; they are suggestive rather than complete. Let each reader and teacher add his own. But the mechanism must become easy before the would-be bowler decides which style he will adopt. Otherwise

XX.--Bowling, third position: bowling arm extended fully forwards and downwards, body facing forwards, back leg fully extended.

[*To face page 61.*

XXI.--Bowling, second position: bowling arm extended fully upwards, body coming round with arm.

[*To face page 61.*

what is naturally easy may be practically uneconomical or risky, as almost every one of my "natural" movements at any game seems to have been. Let the beginner begin without a ball.

a. Notice the extension of the back leg in Hirst's photograh (XX.); that is a simple yet important item. The hand and shoulder are extended fully backwards and downwards.

b. The arm reaches upwards and, in some cases, outwards. Try that, without straining. Having formed the full extension (do not neglect the extra inch that the *shoulder* can give), then point upwards with your first and middle fingers, and, keeping them as far as possible in the same direction, turn the arm round quickly in both ways. It is as if you wished to visit a distant possession of your kingdom and were not content merely to reach it but wished to take an excursion when you had reached it--to become more familiar with it. The top of the stretch will be seen in Ranjitsinhji's book, in the photographs on pp. 76, 79, 90, 99, 101, 104 (First Edition), as well as in the one of Hirst in this volume (XXI.). Abel says:-- "Before you settle on any particular style of bowling, try various plans, and that which is easiest and most effective you should practise continually, but I should strongly recommend the high delivery."

An exception is when you have some good leg-fielders, and dare to imitate W. G.'s effective low action round the wicket.

c. The sideways position of the body during the moment of delivery (see Hirst) seems more usual than the position facing the batsman. This means some of that body-swing which the golfer uses, in common with the tennis-player, the mower, the pitch-forker, and others. It is described in the Volume on Training.

d. After the bowling and (see Hirst), in the case of some experts, before it also, the hand comes right down in front, near the left knee. Let the arm come down from the full upward extension to this position, preserving the outward stretch as long as possible. The shoulder comes with it.

e. The wrist is important. Hold your elbow close to your side, and your palm, fingers upwards, in front of your face, as if you were going to read your own fortune. Then twist it round smartly as far as it will go, the thumb moving across to your left, the little finger away to your right. Recover the first position smartly, and repeat many times. Another wrist-exercise is the one straight up and down. Starting from the first position, bend the hand briskly towards you, as if to fan yourself; then briskly back again.

f. The fingers and thumb, but especially the first finger, must acquire full extensions, full contractions, and the power of rapid yet strong movements in various directions. For example, imagine yourself to be spinning a peg-top with your first finger, now in one direction, now in the other. A second exercise is to move the tips of all the fingers, separately, sharply down towards the palm, and sharply back again.

We need a teacher to tell beginners and others which part of their mechanism is weak or slow, which part is not doing its share of work, which part is working wrongly, and so on.

As a change, the exercises may be applied, *mutatis mutandis,* to left-hand practice.

THE ACTION OF BOWLING

has already been hinted at in these exercises. But, before the ordinary action, may come a few words about the lob, the use of which Mr. Edward Lyttelton advocates so well. The following ideas are mostly his.

We seldom see lob-bowlers to-day. Perhaps many promising boys have been discouraged by too much hitting of their lobs, or too bad fielding (or badly-placed fielding), or too little practice (at a stump and onto a small piece of paper). Yet lobs may be very useful when runs are coming fast; they are like slow twist-services at Tennis or Lawn Tennis--one is ashamed not to kill them. As a change at any time they may pay, since unlike most bowling they break either way and hang.

They must *not* be long hops; they must *not* be too slow. The slowest ball should be the one outside the off-stump, and twisting away. The spin is like that which one gives to a billiard ball with one's fingers; or we might imagine the fingers to be doing to the ball what Pettitt's racket sometimes does in one of his services at Tennis, and Mr. A. W. Gore's in his forehand drive at Lawn Tennis. The high full pitch does not need any spin, except perhaps some drag in the air if one can manage that. The bowling should generally be round the wicket, and have a long run: its exact length should be measured and a mark made where one is to start. A stop must not be made at the crease except in order to vary the pace.

By practising lobs, at games of snob-cricket if not elsewhere, one can learn a great deal about the twist, the pace, the length, the height of the ball for various purposes. It forms an easy apprenticeship. If the bowling be with an indiarubber ball, and the batting be with a stick, then we have excellent practice for batting also, since the indiarubber ball gives confidence to the shrinking right foot and yet receives all the break that is given to it and so encourages the bowler.

The next kind of bowling to learn is the low-action round-arm type, such as W. G. and many of the old cricketers home from India indulge in. It breaks from the leg to the off, coming with the arm as well as with the wrist and perhaps the fingers also. It tempts to leg-hits, and needs good on-side fielding of the kind that E. M. Grace used to show at l*eg.*

Then comes orthodox bowling with the high action, when the needed muscles are well under control. Do not settle on your action--unless you are a genius-bowler--until you have mastered the mechanism. If you do, you may throughout your career fail because some one or more of the important elements have not been brought into the work--perhaps those shoulder-muscles. Stretch your arm up and out and see if it is limber: mine used to be shockingly rigid and cramped. But having exercised the required parts fully and briskly, then find *your* action after experimenting with several. It is not likely that you will be able to bowl well with several actions, though in Tennis I find that at least three utterly different types of service (like those of Saunders or Fairs, Latham or Lambert, and Pettitt) can and almost must be used in the same set. And serving at Tennis is no less elaborate than bowling at Cricket. Indeed the two are closely parallel. At Racquets also I distinguish three or four different actions without appreciable disadvantage. Theoretically I do not see why a moderately good bowler (as distinct from the very best) should not vary his action.

XXII.--Bowling, first position; bowling arm back and down, body facing sideways, weight on back leg.

[*To face page 67.*

We may consider first the medium-paced bowler with a run of let us say five or six yards. This should probably be from a fixed spot, and should not be checked at the wicket except occasionally for the sake of variety of pace. Perhaps the action should begin as it will end, for example with the hand down near the left knee (see Hirst): at Racquets and Tennis I find I serve better--and service here is analogous to bowling at Cricket--if I begin with the position of the racket with which I want to finish up. The principle is *Respice finem*. Others begin with the hand outstretched to the full as it will be at the moment of delivery. These are two plans that are worth trying. Probably the body should be sideways as the bowling starts, not only in order to conceal the ball, but also in order to add the extra body-swing from the hips. And before the arm is lifted it is brought far back and down by many bowlers, as is shown in Photograph XXII., of Hirst. This may be compared with the backward swing of the driver at Golf. Perhaps here, as in Golf, there should be no interval or stop between the swinging back of the hand and the swinging of it forward again for the delivery.

It is generally agreed that the action itself shall be high, somewhat as a server at Lawn Tennis has more chance of serving into the court and well if he takes the ball high in the air: the ball from above--and, as we have said, a man can by daily stretching of shoulder and of arm, of leg and foot, add an inch or two to his bowling stature--comes with more bump, more devilry, more break; is harder to smother, often harder to drive; whereas the low delivery can usually be played forward with safety and confidence (except the W. G. round-arm round the wicket), and is easier to see.

With the delivery let the right hand and shoulder and the head come well forward and downward, the head having previously been back and up, to give full sight of the pitch and batsman.

The back leg, from the hip to the ball of the foot, is stretched at full tension without loss of balance. For there must be immediate recovery in case of a sharp return or a quick run, in which latter case one moves behind the wicket and away from the direction of the stroke. We shall come back to this directly.

We have already suggested how much can be learnt about length and break, etc., from lobs, and about break and drag, etc., from the W. G. action round the wicket. Here we may add that every bowler should be able to bowl round the wicket as well as over it. At first the action is likely to be uncomfortable, and the arrangement of fielders on the leg-side needs care. But bowling round the wicket is almost as good as a complete change; it nearly turns one bowler into two. The batsman has to face differently, and probably he tends to send out his left leg in the wrong direction. I have noticed that, against left-hand round-the-wicket bowlers like Hirst, the batsman generally sends out his left leg far too much towards the left and "away from the batting business" (as Abel calls this fault). Moral: learn to bowl left-hand round the wicket.

As to the *ways of holding the ball,* these actions may at first be tried without a ball at all; to grip a ball would probably cramp the free swing. Let the free swing first be formed. In the same way I found that in Tennis services I got the best training without a racket at all; the actions then went with a pleasant and easy rapidity, until they became habitual at that pace. Then I added the cramping racket-handle, having already acquired freedom as my own. Get correctness and pace and ease before adding anything that might cramp and fetter not only the small extremity, the hand, but also the large basic and motor muscles.

Certainly do not grip the ball before the action; that would tire you and might stiffen your whole apparatus. As a rule, let the tightest grip come just before the very moment of delivery.

There are various grips, of which Photographs XXIII.-XXVI., of Hirst's hand, will show two. A study of these will be more useful than any verbal description. Notice, however, that (1) the little finger is scarcely used at all; (2) the third finger is not always used; (3) the first finger and the thumb do most of the holding and moving; (4) the ball is not held in the palm (except for the sake of a change)[5]; (5) the seam is the part by which the fingers secure their grip and movement (again except for the sake of a change).

The grips can easily become familiar

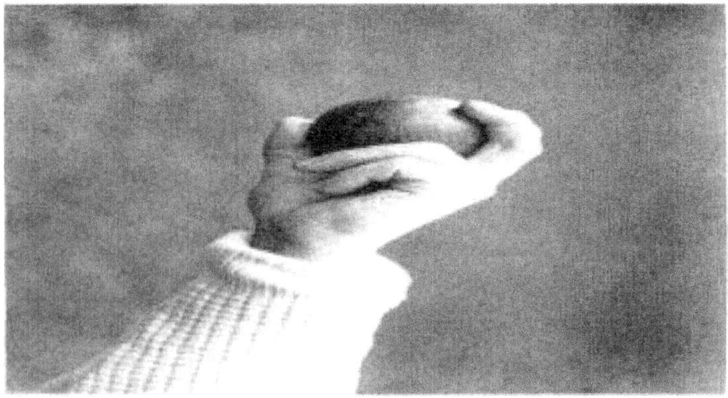

XXIII.--One of Hirst's grips when he bowls: the little finger does not touch the ball, and only the knuckle of the third finger does.

[*Between pages 70 and 71.*

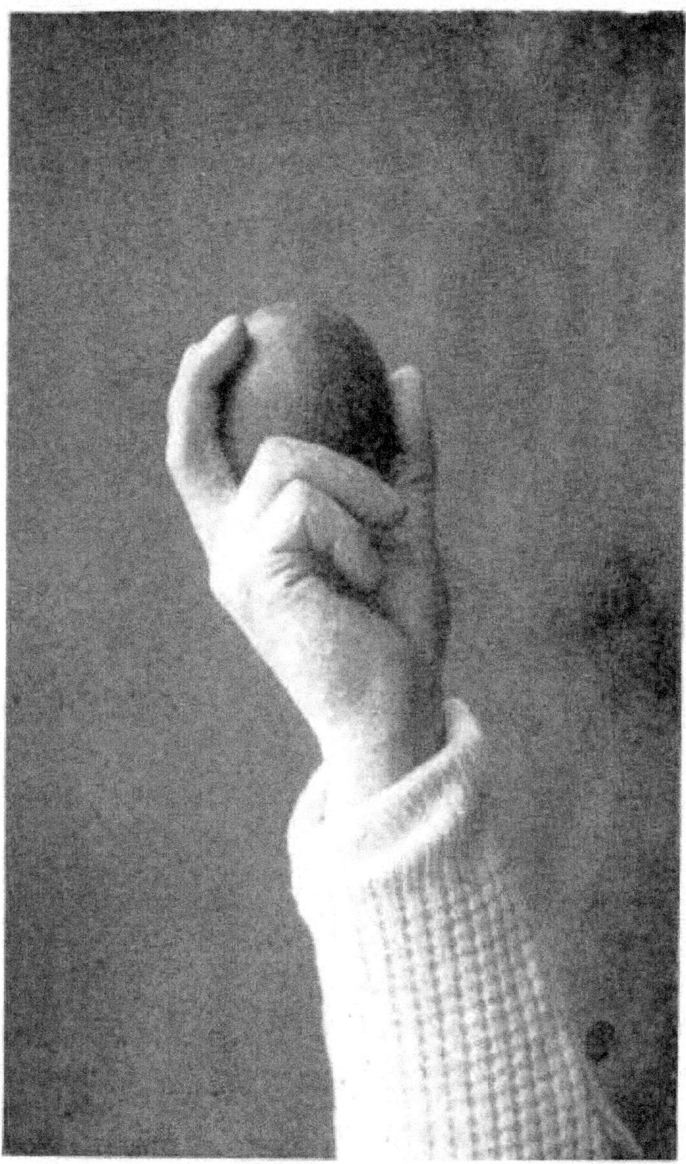

XXIV.--Same grip for right hand bowler.

[*Between pages 70 and 71.*

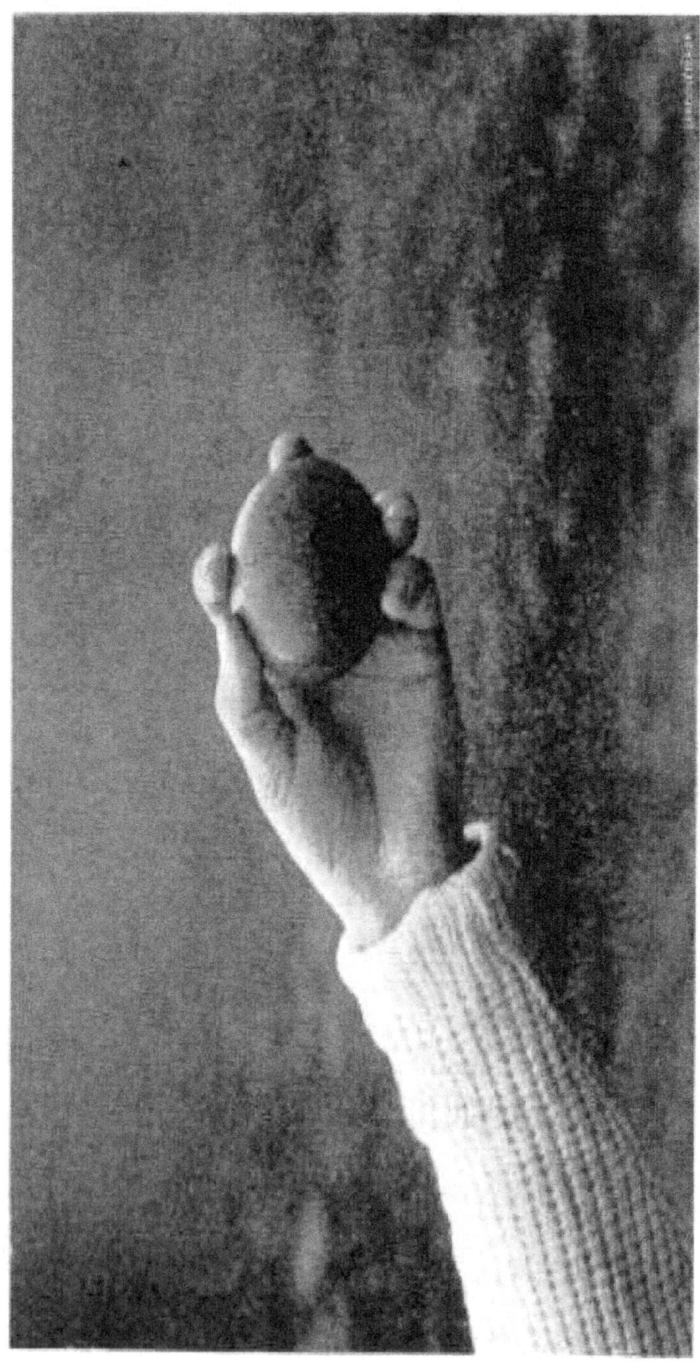

XXV.--Another of Hirst's grips: all the fingers touch the ball, the little one only just with its side.

[*Between pages 70 and 71.*

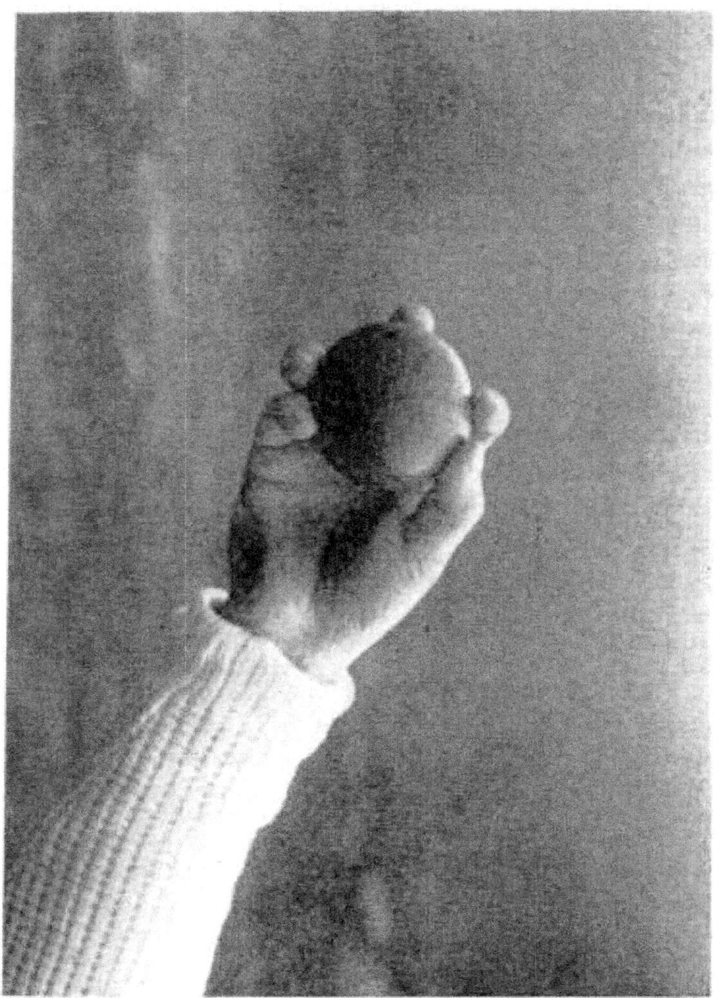

XXVI.--Same grip for right hand bowler.

[*Between pages 70 and 71.*

friends if a ball be held in the hand at odd moments. I recommend a Lawn Tennis ball to begin with, until the fingers become accustomed to the stretching.

Both hands should be trained, just as both right-hand and left-hand actions should be assimilated. The chance of becoming a left-hand bowler (for occasional variety if not regularly) is not one to be missed, especially in these days of billiard-table wickets.

DIRECTION.

The direction should at first be regulated chiefly by the position of the body, especially the feet, and by the larger muscles; without loss of the free swing, however. Aim at a chalk wicket on a wall--an old Lawn Tennis or Squash ball will do to begin with--or try to get someone to stand at the further side of a wicket on a level bit of ground: then you two bowl at that wicket alternately. Correct your mistakes by *exaggerating in the opposite direction* (a principle invaluable for self-correction throughout games and athletics and life). If you are bowling too much to the off-side, then either keep your body turned further to the (batsman's) on-side, or else make your shoulder and arm and hand swing less freely and extendedly and fully to the off, and more fully out to the on. Stretch out and away at the end of the swing, and "follow through." But probably you will be bowling too much to the on; in that case either alter your feet or else make your shoulder and arm and hand swing more fully over and across to the off. For practice, keep it extended out there. Hold it at its extreme limit, and then add another inch to the reach. Exaggerate, but always follow well through. I have never seen this last and most important point mentioned in any book or writing.

Of course in actual practice and play one must be able to bowl persistently to the off. To keep the ball to the off, one must bowl at an imaginary wicket there. One needs the power of forming a picture in the mind's eye. (In Tennis I picture an imaginary net two inches above the real one; that is *my* net, and I ignore the real one.) The reasons why orthodox bowlers bowl to the off are that balls off the wicket are harder to meet in their own line with a straight bat, so long as the right foot is kept rigid. The orthodox bowler has most of his fielders to the off, for catches owing to the crooked bat. If the batsman tries to pull into the desert on the on-side, so as to escape the forest of fielders on the off-side, he generally runs a risk. That is what the bowler wants.

Besides, "it is worth remembering, when bowling to a quick-footed player, that he can run out with more safety to a dead straight ball than to one upon the off. It is very difficult to keep a ball down when it pitches some distance to the side of you." (The writer adds "after a big drive, or after a couple of big drives, it is bad tactics to drop the next ball very short.")

Having acquired a free bowling swing with full extension of hand and arm and shoulder and back muscles and left leg, and in an accurate line towards the imaginary stump on the off-side, one can then learn to vary the line slightly, using for this purpose not only the general direction of the feet and body and arms, but also the smaller movements of the wrist and even of the fingers.

But first get the line safe and sure. Don't yet bother about length or pace or break. Get direction. Concentrate on that.

LENGTH AND HEIGHT.

Though there is no absolutely good length in bowling, yet the following is useful as a general rule:--"For a fast bowler a ball that pitches on a spot within from five to seven yards from the batsman's wicket is 'good-length'; for medium pace, the spot lies between four and five yards; for slow, between three and four yards. Notice that the faster the bowling the wider is the margin of 'good-length.'"

This general rule must be altered according to the state of the ground (wet, dry, etc.), the reach of the batsman, which depends not only on his size but also on his use or non-use of his feet, his "class" (witness the rule, keep a good player playing forward, a bad player playing back), the previous balls which have led up to a certain ball, and so on.

A more comprehensive definition of a good-length ball is that it is just beyond the spot at which a player can play forward with safety, and yet is not a long hop. It is the ball which puts the player in two minds; the ball of which he loses sight; the ball to which he may pay the high compliment of the "half-cock" stroke.

The obvious exceptions are yorkers and full-pitches, which may be excellent balls in due season, and balls to elicit catches.

The yorker is admitted by most authorities to be a useful length to begin with--except with a few batsmen like W. G. It "masquerades" as a full-pitch or half-volley, and succeeds because it is despised as such.

As to the full-pitch, it has several useful varieties. There is the ball which will fall on the top of the wicket--few batsmen like that. Such a ball need not be led up to. Let it be fast, and it is an important unit. It should be frequently practised, after the direction has been mastered. For it is hateful alike to most sloggers, pokers, and well-set batsmen. Then there is the slower full-pitch about the height of the knees. But the fielders must have been carefully placed.

How can one learn to get good lengths--for there are many? How can one learn to use any length at will? For, obviously if the wicket be "plumb," then it may be the bowler's only hope either to keep a fair length and trust in the impatience of human nature, or else to try different lengths.

Bowl a ball lazily, not too high; it will fall short. Bowl another with a full upward stretch of arm and shoulder; you then have a larger circle. If you let the ball go at the right moment, it will not fall short. You can regulate the length, then, by the amount of extension that you employ to give a greater or smaller curve to your hand and the ball, and by the place (within the curve) at which you let the ball go from your hand. While the hand is rising, the sooner you let the ball go the higher that ball will fly; during the downward curve, while the hand is falling, the same is true. Grip the ball till the end of a falling swing, and it may drop quite near to your feet (though there is a swing which scarcely falls at all). The ball which is shorter should generally be bowled a little higher: it was thus that Shaw used often to vary his length and height. He was able to hit any spot on the ground. It is good practice for length and height to put a handkerchief or (later) a small piece of paper or a silver coin now on this spot and now on that, and to make sure of pitching the ball on it with reasonable frequency. The length may be regulated not only by the extension of the arm and hand, and the moment at which one releases the ball, but also by the rest or action of the fingers at this last moment. After one is able to hit a small spot at will, one can bowl for an imaginary spot, just as one can bowl for an imaginary off-wicket.

PACE.

With regard to regulating the pace of the ball, perhaps the medium pace is the best to acquire first. Anyhow, the increase in speed should be gradual. Control of direction and of length should precede control of pace, though it would be impossible to separate the three arts altogether.

In answer to the question of how the pace can be regulated, Mr. Edward Lyttelton writes as follows, with special reference to lobs:--

"There are various ways of doing this. One is to increase the length or speed of your run. It is a plain truth that the pace of the ball depends on the run, as well as on the swing of the arm; as can be verified by observing the impetus given to projectiles thrown from a railway-carriage window. Now the pace of the run up to the crease before the ball leaves the hand is of small importance; the difference depends on the ball being propelled by a body in fast motion or by one hardly moving at all. So you can run fast up to the crease, and, just at the moment of bowling, stop dead. This will give the ball a slow flight, even though your arm moves through the air at its ordinary rate. Or you may take your usual number of strides, but each a little longer than usual. This gives extra speed to the run, and consequently to the ball, but the batsman can hardly perceive the reason why. His eyes are fixed on the bowler's arm. Lastly, there is the trick of giving the ball a forward spin with the tips of the fingers as it leaves the hand, which causes a fast bound from the pitch. Combined with a fast run, this spin makes a ball come along at a surprising pace, without the arm doing anything out of the common. Certain it is that very few lob-bowlers study the run up to the wicket sufficiently. It ought not to be mechanically uniform."

Slow bowling, as Mr. A. G. Steel points out, may have numerous advantages. It may curve in the air. The batsman has to hit with more force, with more risk of hitting up, more chance of being stumped if he runs out, more chance of being caught at the wicket; the slow bowler has greater control over the pitch of the ball and its spin; he can recover his balance so quickly and so thoroughly that himself he becomes an extra man in the field, having plenty of time to stop a drive and to get behind and put down the wicket when the ball is thrown on; he can last longer.

But he must pitch the ball further up, nearer to the batsman's reach; he may be hit hard and placed anywhere unless he can make his ball hang in the air or otherwise deceive the batsman, as when the bowler sends it from the palm of the hand, not from the fingers.

Slow medium bowling is safer; and as a general rule medium bowling should be practised before very slow or very fast be attempted. Perhaps for most ordinary bowlers it should form the staple pace, so easily can it be made a little faster or a little slower. It has this advantage over very slow bowling: that it need not be pitched so far up. It has this advantage over very fast bowling, that it can use the break both ways, and can be kept up without much fatigue. He who bowls well within his pace runs little risk of straining himself, although every now and then (like the slow bowler) he can put in an occasional fast ball for a change. No one should ever bowl so fast as to endanger the swing and the knack, as so many boys do; or so fast that he dare not return to the slower for the silly fear of being hit.

Nevertheless--as I once heard a coach remark--if you're a fool perhaps you'd better bowl fast.

Pace may be varied, somewhat as length may be varied (see above); for example, by a longer or shorter, quicker or slower run; by a run arrested; by a quicker or slower or arrested movement of some part of the mechanism--shoulder, wrist, etc. Spofforth used to hold the ball loosely for slow bowling, tightly for fast, as if he were a train which gives an impetus to the jumping-off passenger by holding on to him till the last moment. Spofforth's pace as a rule was medium rather than very fast.

BREAK, SPIN, CURL, ETC.

Anyone who has practised bowling in this order--mastering direction, then length, then pace, will now wish to add some sort of break, as the baseball pitcher wishes to add some sort of curl. But here again, as with pace, it is a great error to acquire in excess, so as to "endanger the knack." I remember a boy who got into his school XI. at the end of the term simply because he could put on a huge break. He had no other merits; in his only match he failed miserably. As a high authority says:--

"The best ball is not the one that breaks most but the one that just breaks enough--enough to beat the bat but not the wicket, or else enough to beat the centre of the bat and just touch its edge."

The general mechanism of the break has been best described by Mr. A. G. Steel in his now classical chapter of the "Badminton Volume":--

"The spin or rotary motion from right to left is gained by grasping the ball chiefly with the thumb and the first and second fingers, the third and fourth fingers being placed altogether round the other side of the ball. The moment the ball leaves the hand, the latter is turned quickly over from right to left, and at the same time the first and second fingers and the thumb, coming over with the hand, impart a powerful twist to the ball, which leaves the hand when the latter is turned palm downwards. There is also, at the time of delivery, an outward and upward movement of the elbow, which gives the arm the shape of a curve, or almost a semicircle. The ball goes on its way spinning rapidly from right to left, and the moment it touches the ground twists very sharply toward the off side of the batsman. This ball (termed in cricket parlance the 'leg break'), when well bowled, is perhaps one of the most deadly of all balls, but it is also the most difficult for a bowler to master. It is always a slow ball, as to bowl it fast with any accuracy of pitch is an impossibility; at any rate, it may be assumed to be so, as no bowler has ever yet appeared who could bowl it otherwise than slow.... There are some slow bowlers who have become fairly proficient at it, and who have enjoyed at various times--especially against batsmen they had never met before--a certain amount of success; but it is a style of bowling which should be encouraged only to the extent of enabling every bowler to use it occasionally."

There are at least three different kinds of break; they may be combined in various ways. The American baseball pitching is developed to a higher point of skill than our bowling, and can probably teach us not a few lessons.

(1.) The first break is called the natural break; it is usually from the off to the leg (from the leg to the off in the case of the left-hand bowler). It comes almost or quite of its own accord with the action itself; indeed one can scarcely ever bowl a ball without *some* action-break, any more than one can easily hit a billiard ball without any break. This kind is often called the break "with the arm."

(2.) The wrist-break cannot be altogether separated from this; some such break also is almost natural if not inevitable.

(3.) The third kind is the finger-break (including the thumb-break). It is a spin given at the last moment. The fingers move round in one direction or in the other, *the first finger* being as a rule the most important factor. This finger needs to be exercised by itself. When one looks at a professional bowler's hands one finds this finger especially hardened or worn or blistered.

The finger-break (with some wrist-break) can be partly given by the grip itself. Hirst's two grips in the photographs should be carefully studied and imitated. C. T. B. Turner, the great Australian, used to bowl quite a different ball according to the special grip. Shrewsbury tells of a match in which the Notts wickets fell before Turner, because the men did not notice the change of grip. Shrewsbury noticed it, and did not fall a victim. The middle and third fingers were sometimes bent not round the ball, but in upon the palm of the hand. Again, the spin will be absent or lessened if the ball be held, not by the seam, as it usually is, but by its ordinary skin. For the American baseball grip with a view to curl in the air (and also affecting twist off the ground) see below.

The least important finger is the little finger; then comes the third finger.

The break can be partly given by this or that special movement of fingers and thumb, or chiefly fingers, during the moment when the ball leaves the hand. The effect of the varied grip, upon pace, has already been described. There are the over-spins for extra pace; the drag-spins;

and the side-spins. Every billiard player will realise what these terms mean.

The balls with arm-and wrist-and finger-breaks do not come off the ground in the same way; the right-hand bowler's artificial (wrist and finger) break from the leg to the off will have a different effect from the left-hand bowler's "natural" break from the leg to the off. And results vary also according to the wicket, the wet and slippery (as distinct from the drying and caking wicket) scarcely imparting any break at all; there is no "bite."

The commonest break (of the right-hand bowler) is from the off to the *leg*. Most bowlers and throwers have it. It is often said that the reverse-break, from the leg to the off, is impossible as a safe and reliable ball for a fast bowler, except in so far as it comes with the action of bowling. Be this as it may--and I see no anatomical reason for the impossibility--the leg-break is easy for a medium or slow bowler, and is especially effective round the wicket, as many old bowlers have frequently proved. Mr. A. G. Steel's excellent description of the action must be quoted from the "Badminton Volume":

"The ball was delivered round the wicket, at the very extent of the crease, in order to make the angle from the hand to an imaginary straight line between the two middle stumps as great as possible. The hand was very little higher than the hip when the ball was delivered, and instead of the hand and wrist being completely turned over at the moment of delivery, as in the slow leg-break, the fingers imparted a right to left spin to the ball. The ball, coming from a great distance round the wicket and with a considerable amount of leg-spin, would be gradually working away to the batsman's off-side every inch of its journey, both before and after pitching."

Such a break would be liable to lead to a catch at the wicket or in the slips. It is especially useful in school cricket. School bowlers--and others--should acquire this action. It is not difficult or exhausting, but it needs a careful study of field-placing on the on-side.

(4.) To the break given by arm, wrist, and fingers, we may now add the curl, which some bowlers have or occasionally have, but which few if any bowlers know how to teach. The following remarks about the American baseball-pitcher's curl in the air, produced *by a throw*, are worth studying. They are from Mr. Walter Camp's "Book of College Sports." I think I am right in saying that the American curve usually does not come till towards the end of the ball's flight.

"The easiest curve, and the one to be acquired first, is the out-curve. The simplest method is to take the ball in the hand between the extended thumb and the first and second fingers, the third and little fingers being closed. The ball rests against the (side of the) middle part of the third finger, but is firmly clasped by the first two and the thumb. If the arm be then extended horizontally from the shoulder, with the palm of the hand up, it will be seen that if the ball were spun like a top by the two fingers and thumb it would turn in the way indicated by the arrow in the diagram. This is the way it must twist to accomplish the out-curve. The simpler way to impart this twist is not the spinning motion, but rather a snap as the ball is leaving the fingers, performed almost entirely without the aid of the thumb. The sensation is that of throwing the ball hard, but dragging it back with the ends and sides of the fingers just as it leaves the hand." For further instructions the reader should consult this excellent work, published by the Century Company of New York.

The writer goes on to remark:--

"The most logical explanation of the curvature of a ball depends upon the supposition of the compression of the air just in front of the ball and a corresponding rarefaction immediately behind it, so that the ball by its friction is deflected from its true course."

It is interesting to notice that, in contrast with our "batting versus bowling" problem, "in spite of all restrictions, such is the growing skill of pitchers that the problem is constantly under discussion how to legislate in favour of the batsmen."

(5.) Additional curl or break may be added by the wind, slope of the ground, and so on.

In all cases, the break must be given especially at the last moment, and must not be expended in the previous action, unless the object be to deceive the batsman. Obviously one should not always put on the same amount of break; one should appear to do so. A straight ball following many breaks from the off is apt to be very effective.

Now as to the learning of the break, two or three notions seem to me sheer common sense.

(1.) The muscles of the various mechanisms, and especially of the wrist and fingers, must be exercised in various ways: by full extensions in different directions, by full contractions, by partial movements in different directions, and so on. A certain amount of strength is needed, but let litheness not be sacrificed.

(2.) Underhand bowling of breaks in either direction not only exercises these mechanisms, and makes them habitual and easy, but it also shows effects very clearly. Stump-cricket with an indiarubber ball and underhand bowling is good training for the bowler's break as well as for the batsman's straight bat.

(3.) Slow bowling is fine for the same reasons. During it the ball is held longer in the fingers; after it the ball is "held" longer by the ground. Hence it also shows its effects clearly and encourages the beginner. Moreover, the slow breaking ball is useful as a change for the medium-paced bowler. Some of the break thus acquired as an easy habit may be transferred to medium or fast bowling.

Concealment is of the utmost importance. The extra Commandment, "Thou shalt not be found out," is of great moment when once the bowler has control of the ball's flight and spin.

To hide direction is hard, unless the curl be used. To hide length and pace, as Shaw, Spofforth, Lohmann and others used to, is easier: one or two helps have been offered above. We may notice that Shaw used to alter the height of his hand: this had several important results; for example, the low delivery made the ball bump less and "skim" more. Shaw again would bowl a very effectively concealed variety, a ball *rather* shorter, *rather* slower, *rather* higher. A great change is not usually so effective as a small one, except when a very slow or medium bowler occasionally bowls a very fast ball. In masking these changes, as well as the break, the bowler needs what

XXVII.--Bowler waiting for ball to be thrown in: he is standing well back from the wicket.

[*To face page 91.*

Mr. A. G. Steel alludes to as the wiliness of the serpent with the apparent harmlessness of the dove. He needs complete mastery of this or that part of the mechanism by itself, so that he may or may not turn his wrist or fingers at the last moment either completely or partially, but anyhow "with intent to deceive." Need a skilful bowler be a skilful liar?

The art of *taking balls at the wicket,* like the art of fielding balls, demands a rapid recovery of balance. After his effort the bowler must either field the ball or else get ready with his wicket between himself and the fielder. As the photograh (XXVII.) of Hirst shows, he should not stand too near the wicket, for it is easier to move forward than to move back. He must also be prepared for a bad throw, either too high or else too low--perhaps a half-volley or what would be to a batsman a "good length" ball.

The "Badminton Volume" gives this useful advice:--"A golden rule for every bowler to observe is--after the batsman has played the ball, get back to the wicket as quickly as possible. Neglect of this rule loses many a 'run-out.' If a bowler does not get back to his wicket, there is no one to take the ball and knock the bails off should the batsman run and the ball be returned to the bowler's end. When the ball is thrown up, the bowler should not take it till it has just passed the wicket; he should then seize and sweep the ball into the stumps in one and the same action."

For the purpose of taking the ball and putting down the wicket rapidly--in fact almost by a single movement--he cannot do better than practise wicket-keeping now and then. This should give him hints for bowling also. It should help him to keep his real eye on the ball and his imaginary eye, his mind's eye, on imaginary wickets. He must sense by imagination, and by "feel," precisely where the wickets are, just as at Tennis. I have to sense where the "Grille" or "Dedans" is, even while my real outward eye is on the ball.

The bowler, like the wicket-keeper, should be an adviser (but with judgment and tact) to the captain, especially with regard to the throwing in and backing up by this or that fielder, and the correct placing of all the fielders, which must depend on circumstances and individual batsmen. This has brought us to more general remarks on bowling.

GENERAL HINTS.

The first and foremost piece of advice to the would-be bowler, that is to say to every cricketer, is to read what the great authorities, Messrs. A. G. Steel, Ranjitsinhji, Grace, the Lytteltons, and others say about the importance of bowling, and of learning to bowl well or better, not only for the sake of the game's future and of the team's success, but also for the sake of personal enjoyment. Let the reader digest what Mr. Edward Lyttelton says about practice in the bedroom, and what Mr. C. B. Fry (in the "Strand" for July, 1902) says about the helps which he used to his grand athletic success--for instance, kicking a small ball in a courtyard, and jumping over an arm-chair. Let every cricketer read how the Americans train for baseball. Then let him not despise the mastering of the mechanism in his bedroom or elsewhere, if possible before a large looking-glass. There should be one or two in every pavilion.

The following advice is not new, but it will all bear repetition. No amount of honest care spent in suggestions about bowling can be considered as wasted. The future of enjoyable cricket lies largely with improvement in bowling.

Be able to bowl round as well as over the wicket, for such a change of starting-point is almost as good as a change of action. In view of what certain Americans have achieved in Philadelphia and elsewhere by being taught the use of the left side (for drawing, modelling, etc.) in early childhood, I do not hesitate to say, learn to bowl fairly well with the left hand as well as with the right. The control of the left side would add power to batting and fielding even if it led to little success in actual bowling.

When you have got the direction and *can* bowl persistently to the off, practise the straight and fast yorker as well as the good length ball to the off. In fact, practise intentional variety; do not rely on the variety which is incidental to careless and "undisciplined" bowling.

You must have firm feet--the left foot must have nails that bite the ground well, especially near the boot's toe; you must have strong hands--they may be hardened by salt, etc., or, in case of sore places, may be protected by adhesive plaister round the finger or hand (this prevents painful friction). Sprains may be treated by water or massage or radiant light and heat.

Having attended to such things, study pitches--their soft or hard spots, the trees, etc., behind the bowler's arm, the direction of the sun, of the wind--in fact, all details that a careful general *must* notice. Spofforth used to make a point of finding out "the pace of the wicket, even if his first effort cost him dear." One or two balls just off the pitch, before play begins, may save such runs. Don't bowl these or the early ones too fast; the Public School Racquet representatives at Queen's slash about from the very moment that they enter the court. This is silly. Start gently; increase the severity by degrees.

At the beginning of an innings or of a new batsman's innings pitch the ball well up. A yorker is among the most effective attacks (except to W. G. and a few others); even a half-volley is often useful, or a full-pitch on the body, but *not* a long hop.

Correct your mistakes of direction, length, and so on, by exaggerating a little in the opposite direction.

To a slogger a straight ball--unless it be a yorker--is not the best, as a rule, especially if he runs out; a ball to the off may be most useful, for a slogger generally runs out straight down the pitch rather than towards the side (in which case he would turn an off-ball into a straight ball). With W. G.'s action round the wicket, a ball on the leg-side may be just the thing. A break to the off is generally needed, so as to tempt a catch to cover or third man.

Do not mind having your "head-balls" hit. Mr. A. G. Steel's words must be borne in mind constantly, at least for ordinary occasions when the main object is not to keep the runs down. He says:--"When a bowler is put on to bowl by his captain, it is his duty to do everything in his power to dislodge the batsman. It is really quite a secondary consideration for him whether many or few runs are being made off his bowling." As a sequel to this, he urges that "a slow bowler should try every wile that can possibly be attempted. By adopting slow bowling he has undertaken to use 'the wisdom of the serpent' in the guise of the 'harmlessness of the dove,' and has sacrificed pace to cunning and thought."

If the bowler be very brave, he will feed the strong stroke of the batsman. I often find this plan effective in Racquets and Tennis. The opponent tries "just one too many," or tries to excel beyond his ability. But of course it would be a greater error to forget the fieldmen's poor hands and to bowl the batsman into practice and sure sight, than it would be to bowl merely for maidens, unless the other bowler is playing ninepins with the stumps, or unless defensive bowling is required at the close finish to a match, or in order to excite a batsman to impatience.

Most experiments should have been already made at the nets or in practice-games. It is there that you should learn how to lead up to a killing ball, as the Lawn Tennis or Chess player does, rather than always to spring the very best on the batsman at once. To plan each ball deliberately beforehand, to let each have a definite purpose, involves not only these previous trials, but also a good memory, an absence of hurry, a refusal to despair.

Despair is almost natural when chances have been missed. I remember a season of College Cricket during which I got about 130 wickets, and had over 60 chances missed. I had to console myself by imagining each chance--mostly to the sleepy slips--to be a wicket. That may console one slightly.

Another consolation is to remember that each fresh batsman is a fresh beginning to the game. He comes in unready, a hope to the bowler.

Observation and memory have been invaluable helps to me at my own games. I translate my experiences into Cricket language. From behind the wicket and elsewhere, observe the commonest hits off the commonest balls with this or that break, especially when the batsman shapes thus or thus. Observe how the poking potterer is dismissed by the high full-pitch or by the ball to entice a catch in the slips--for him you will note in your mind, "Two short slips and perhaps two square legs." Watch the fingers of the nervous batsman grip the bat tight; watch the feet and body shuffle in anxiety; watch the feeble strokes that result; watch the balls that worry him most before he gets confidence.

The weak point of a batsman should be the point of most frequent attack, and that weak point may differ on different days, and according to the individual batsman's special frame of mind. "Ah," I have often thought when I faced an old opponent, "if only I could tell your strongest and weakest strokes *to-day and now*! Will you be slow on your legs now? Will you neglect that right foot, oh, mine enemy?"

Observe whether the batsman himself is intelligent and observant, or--what generally amounts to the same thing--practised to the verge of automatism. Do not assume that every batsman will notice everything that you are doing. Excessive wiliness is often wasted.

Observe how a player with a certain "stance" will tend to show a certain fault--as to draw away his right foot. Classify players in groups. Then when the hitherto new and "unseen" batsman arrives, you may start at an advantage; you may save yourself unnecessary experimentation.

Make notes of these and other "tips." Cricket is as well worth notes as Tennis and Racquets, and my notes for these games have proved of yeoman service in matches. "How they would give my whole show away!" was the remark of an American player. "Yes," I replied, "if anyone had the patience to use them, he might very soon beat me." Work out theories; remember the keenness of Spofforth, who lay awake at nights plotting and planning. Such imaginations are good for the intellect and (in an obvious way) "a very present help in time of trouble." Read, observe, ask pros., veterans, wicket-keepers. Make notes, recollect, use. Judge by results.

For instance, work out where you will want this and that fielder placed. Most books give excellent diagrams: Ranjitsinhji's are the fullest. But do not be tied down by any such diagram. Be ready to change the positions--by a word or a movement of the hand--according to individual grounds, days, batsmen, and so on.

One need not confine one's practice to the nets and games. These are indispensable in their place, but not self-sufficient. Practice with a smaller and softer ball is not to be despised; it will give one freer movements, more obvious effects in break, and thus more knowledge and confidence. And one should do the special exercises--and others devised by wiser heads than mine--before one dares to despair. One must first master the mechanisms, try several actions, practise with a friend (putting a stump between oneself and him, and bowling at it alternately with him, a third enthusiast acting as wicket-keeper), practise needless variety (with wrist or fingers stiff or loose, and so on). One can give oneself every chance, every benefit of the doubt. It was years before I learnt to serve at Racquets or Tennis. I am not nearly at my best yet.

When one is at the nets, one must be independent. One must imagine oneself bowling in actual overs. One must notice where each ball, sent with a special purpose, is generally hit. In my practice of Cricket I never did this; in my practice of my own games I do it with marked results.

Boys should certainly practise, even if they do not regularly play, with a smaller ball, a smaller bat, a shorter pitch. I wish that the M.C.C. Committee would study the expressed opinions of Messrs. A. G. Steel, Ranjitsinhji, Grace and others--elicit the hitherto unexpressed opinions of other experts; discuss the matter, and then, if it seemed good, issue an *authoritative advice* to schoolmasters and others, urging the use of adapted ball, bat, and pitch. Though any one single measure would not suit all, yet it would be convenient, and would be a step in the right direction. Let there be light and small bats and balls.

It would be well also if old players would tell the young player to practise lobs, to try the W. G. action round the wicket, to master the mechanisms of ordinary overhand bowling, to avoid excessive pace, and break; to practise at the nets as if he were bowling in an actual game, only with more experimentation--to bowl an over, then have a rest; to make notes; to work out theories; to be keen. A few words from a famous expert come with a thousand times more force than any amount of advice from the present writer, even though the latter be stating only most obvious and incontrovertible truths. For the word of a successful man availeth much.

CHAPTER III.

FIELDING AND THROWING-IN.

THE future of Cricket lies less perhaps with reform of the game itself than with more adequate preparation for play, so that each part of each department of it may be better done--done with more skill, more enjoyment, more profit. And of all departments fielding needs most care and favour. It must become so good and so interesting as to be a pride and a pleasure, instead of--as it now is--a dulness and a drudgery.

The first requisite will be to realise that fielding is complex. Whereas Cricket is often called a trinity of games, of which one member is fielding, fielding itself, though regarded as a single occupation, involves a multitude of arts and too often a multitude of sins. Quite apart from the different qualities demanded for different places in the field, all fielders alike should possess certain characteristics in common. In this chapter we shall speak of fielding in general, referring the reader to the books by Ranjitsinhji and others for special and exceptional information about special places. Thus short slip may have to be ready not to move his feet but merely to shift his weight, whereas cover must be ready to do both.

A few minutes' study of the photographs of Hirst and Shrewsbury, and of an actual or imaginary game, will show that as a rule many virtues are needful. Ranjitsinhji gives the following nine Commandments:--

"There are certain rules which apply to all fieldsmen, viz.:--

1. Keep the legs together when the ball is hit straight to you and while you are picking it up.

2. Always back up the man who is receiving the ball at the wicket, when it is thrown in, but not too close.

3. Always try for a catch, however impossible it may seem.

4. Always be on the look-out and ready to start.

5. Run at top speed, but not rashly, the moment the ball is hit.

6. Use both hands whenever possible.

7. Do not get nervous if you make a mistake.

8. Obey your captain cheerfully and promptly.

9. Never be slack about taking up the exact position assigned to you; never move about in an aimless, fidgetty manner."

These Commandments apply to the whole side, since, as has been well said, "In a true sense, the strength of a fielding side must be measured by its weakest member, as that of a chain is measured by its weakest link. Then, again, when there is a really bad fielder on a side, more balls seem to go to him than to any one else. Put him where you will, he seems to attract the ball."

Let the reader fancy himself fielding at cover. What must be his habits?

He must be ready to back up the wicket-keeper.

He must be ready to start at once in any direction either with his legs or with his arm or with both.

He must time the ball; he must also anticipate, his foreknowledge being based on instinct, observation, and memory.

He may have to run and to run hard.

He may have to move his hands, or one of them, rapidly and accurately towards the ball's line of flight; this may involve a bending of trunk, and an extension of limbs for stooping and stretching.

He must preserve or immediately recover balance.

He must be able to draw back his hands, or one of them, the instant that the ball has touched them or it. This yielding movement must be timed to a nicety.

He must grasp the ball either as a catch or as a ball to be thrown in.

In the latter case he must decide to which end, at what pace, etc., he will throw it in.

He must then throw it in accurately. This last rule of fielding alone postulates a special and difficult art.

Having found out what is to be practised, the would-be fielder must realise that the practice as well as the fielding itself are abundantly worth while. "That side would have been out for a third of the score if one or two of us in our palmy days had been in the field," remarked a veteran spectator at a big match. This was quite true--catches were missed, and they were costly enough. Ranjitsinhji says, "As to the importance of good fielding, it is easy to prove it. Each catch that is missed simply adds another batsman to the opposite side. If five catches are dropped, the side that drops them has to all intents and purposes fifteen men to dispose of instead of ten." Besides the chances, there were the balls not anticipated, not stopped, not thrown in smartly, not thrown in accurately. The so-called "safe" fielders often lost a run by their safe waiting. "Patient waiting no loss" is a bad rule. Mr. Edward Lyttelton laments this inferiority. What a contrast to Mr. V. K. Royle, whose *habit* was to stand like a man ready to sprint in any direction, even before the ball had been hit. Such a man either ran the batsman out or else saved run after run by sheer terrorism; he did not slack off merely because he thought the ball might possibly not come near him. He seemed to be convinced that it certainly would come not necessarily *to* him but for him to field. He was the ideal. And W. G. tells us of another: "My brother Fred and Jupp used to go after everything and try for every catch, *as if the match depended on their individual efforts*; and the extraordinary results which followed surprised others as well as themselves. There is no finer sight in the cricket field than a brilliant fieldsman doing his utmost; and every feat that he performs meets with quick and hearty recognition by the spectators." Such examples and words make one feel that keenness and skill and success *are* worth while. The alertness and rapidity with accuracy are qualities for character and for life as well as for cricket.

After the complexity of fielding and its importance have been realised, the next thing is to improve fielding. Why has it not been cultivated as a piece of land that may become fruitful? Partly perhaps because the fielder is not mentioned on the scoring-sheet (except for the catches, which go chiefly to the bowler's credit); partly because the long-sided practice-nets render most fielding unnecessary; partly because fielders are not keen, and that means because they do not field scientifically. Fielding is regarded as a subsidiary and slavish drudgery, not as an important and fine art. And now for a few possible remedies of a general character, to be supplemented by others and by special training for special places in the field.

Every fielder should practise all-round fielding, while he makes one particular place (or two) his speciality: the choice of this place should depend on the mental as well as the physical qualities--on smart readiness, power of extension, and so forth.

He should study the commonest hits to his place, learning the curves and breaks which the ball will most frequently show.

He *must* be alert. Let me here quote Mr. Edward Lyttelton's excellent remarks:--"Unless strong measures are taken, the school-fieldsmen will stand on their heels, while the ball is being hit; and this is generally the cause of that heart-sickening want of life--that imperturbable middle-aged decorum which is so often to be noticed among boy-cricketers of seventeen, eighteen, nineteen years of age, and is enough, when seen, to make old cricketers weep. But not to stand on the heels requires effort and stimulus; and it is astonishing how often you may make the effort and reap no reward; the ball doesn't come. But when it does, what a change! The leap, the determination that the batsman shall not score, the racing after the ball, are all part of the same dash which must begin from the toes, not from the heel. Now some of these early principles can be taught to a boy by taking him singly, and throwing or hitting the ball, not too hard, either at him or to one side just within his utmost reach; and, by constant encouragement and exhortation, the trainer may induce him again and again to do violence to his propriety, in the first place, and then to stretch his sinews and curve his backbone till he finds himself capable of a brilliancy which he never before suspected. The exercise is terrific, and ten minutes *per diem* are amply sufficient. It is best to take only one at a time. No one can guess the improvement that is sure to ensue if this regime is faithfully observed.... A deep field is standing with his whole body ready to jump in any direction that may be required. There comes a catch, but it is very doubtful if he can get to it; only because he was ready to start he does so, and perhaps the best bat on the side walks home; or, owing to the same fact, he again and again saves a ball from going to the boundary. Now, if this is the case with a deep field, how much more with cover-point and other 'save one' fields!"

He must notice and practice several waiting-positions, taking good fielders as his models. Whichever he decides to use, he must not stand on his heels. Fielders refuse to learn the art of readiness; so does our nation in its daily life. It is the prompt readiness not to go in one direction only, but to go in *any* direction, perhaps backwards, without loss of poise and self-control--for the hands must be prepared to be extended anywhere, and at the end of the extension to grasp securely. So far from such an alertness being a common sight, an inalienable possession of most players, it is as rare as open-mindedness. There is only one thing rarer in fielding, and this is the custom of anticipating strokes, though heaven knows that similar strokes have been repeated often enough to be observed and remembered! But "education" does not encourage observation.

In addition to the readiness to get at the ball, there must be the readiness to back up.

The fielder must follow each ball. If he finds this dull, let him pretend that he is the fielder to whom the ball has been sent; let him field it in his imagination.

In a bedroom or elsewhere he may practice stoopings and extensions (as in Photograph XXVIII. of Hirst), a yielding of the hands and a rapidly closed grip at the end of the extensions. All the common attitudes and movements for stopping and receiving balls may be acquired outside the field. The muscles must be familiarised with their future work; for, as Mr. Lyttelton says, "If every field picked up and threw in as quickly as his knee joints and the state of his arm allowed him, a very considerable percentage of the runs usually scored would be saved."

Catching may be learnt with a soft ball against a wall or in games of catch. The hands should be held not too far apart nor too far from the body. Both hands should be used, if possible. The difficulty is to judge the flight, to time the instant to draw back just enough--for "he must learn to let the ball come into his hands as into an Aunt Sally's mouth. It is entirely wrong to grab or snap at it"--and then to hold tight. There are brought into play the senses of sight, of hearing--different sounds accompany different hits, and in Racquets I get much help from what my ear tells me--and of touch, as well as of other faculties.

As practice for stopping balls, wicket-keeping

XXVIII.--Fielding a low ball with one hand: the opposite leg is fully extended.

[*To face page 112.*

is good except for the feet. It teaches one to bend quickly, to extend quickly; it cultivates pluck and patience and observation, since the wicket-keeper must stand firm and wait and watch each ball if he hopes not to be hurt.

Every cricketer--I would go so far as to say every ordinary human being--should learn and practise throwing-in. Dr. Grace says that the player "should practise picking-up and throwing-in underhand." At first this should be acquired as a separate accomplishment, till it can be incorporated and nearly ingrafted into the action of fielding, so that the whole process may become, as it were, a single movement started half-unconsciously by the sight of a batsman preparing to strike. The right action for throwing will be dealt with directly.

Interesting matches will do much to improve the keenness about fielding and therefore the care given to it. It is mainly because the American School and University baseball matches *are* so interesting, so absorbing, that good fielding is so sedulously sought after. We might arouse and sustain interest by variety; personally I should like to see handicap-matches occasionally introduced. A few kinds are suggested in another chapter. Tip-and-run is excellent training for the batsman as well for the fielders and wicket-keeper.

Subsidiary games and exercises are also essential. In these, as in matches, there should either be prizes or--as Mr. Edward Lyttelton advises--"the players should be encouraged to compete for colours to wear, which need consist of nothing further than a cap of well-marked hue. There is no reason to underrate the power of this enticement. Human beings have ever been addicted to ornament, and some have thought that great wars have been fought for very little else than the difference between one colour and another. It is quite certain that the authorization of caps for proficiency in cricket does wonders; and it is a stimulus quite innocent enough to be worth trying." The same writer goes on to suggest that "it ought to be possible to devise a means of a social practice of fielding, which without involving the waste of time of ordinary match fielding, would ensure to each individual something to do, and some stimulus to do it."

We might with advantage study American

XXIX.--Fielding, second position: the hand drawn back behind the ear somewhat further back than most American Baseball fielders prefer.

[*To face page 114.*

methods of practice, not with a view to slavish copying, but with a view to adapted borrowing. Mr. Walter Camp thus describes the method and apparatus for improving the accuracy of height and of direction; after remarking that "every one has what may be called a natural way of throwing the ball, but this so-called natural 'way' usually means a perverted method acquired through carelessness, or attempts to throw too hard before the arm is sufficiently accustomed to the work," he points out such faults as to return the ball before the recovery of balance. He then goes on thus: "To get an idea of the first steps towards the acquisition of this method, let the player take the ball in his hand, and, bringing it back level with his ear, planting both feet firmly, attempt to throw the ball without using the legs or body. At first the throw is awkward and feeble, but constant practice speedily results in moderate speed and peculiar accuracy. After steady practice at this until quite a pace is acquired, the man may be allowed to use his legs and body to increase the speed, still, however, sticking to the straight-forward motion of the hand, wrist, and the arm.... There is no delay caused by drawing back the arm past the head or by turning the body around, which loses so much valuable time. Its accuracy is due to the fact that it is easier to aim at an object with a hand in front of the eyes than when it is out (to the side) beyond the shoulder. One can easily ascertain this by comparing the ease of pointing the index finger at any object when the hand is in front of the face, with the difficulty of doing so when the arm is extended out sideways from the body. Still further, in the almost round-arm throwing, which many players use, the hand describes an arc, and the ball must be let go at the proper point to go true. If let go at any other point in the swing, the throw is certain to be wild.... The majority of the best throwers in the country use principally the fore-finger and middle finger in giving direction to the ball." Mr. Camp then describes the system of hitting to a number of fielders--this is to be found in some English Schools, but in America the practisers take it in turn to hit to the others, "the batter being able to knock high flies, line hits, long flies, and occasionally a sharp hot grounder; a good man, while avoiding running the men to death, will

XXX.--Waiting for a catch: elbows ready to draw back slightly the moment the ball touches the hands.

[*Between pages 116 and 117.*

XXXI.--A one-handed catch: body bent slightly back from the hips.

[*Between pages 116 and 117.*

occasionally give each man an opportunity to make a brilliant catch. Nothing encourages and improves the candidates so much as keeping their ambition thoroughly aroused during the entire time of practice." "Exercise that toughens the hands--such as swinging on the flying-rings, or rope-climbing--is found to be useful." "The work with the boxing gloves is designed to improve the man's general muscular development, make him quick and firm upon his feet, and rapid in judgment and action." "On the running-track, the men take a few turns to limber up, and then practise quick starting, and short, sharp spurts at full speed, rather than the more leisurely, long-continued run of the men who are training for boating honours." "The sliding-spool is an admirable device for cultivating the muscles used in throwing. (The spool is a piece of wood, like a large reel of cotton, moving upon a rope tied, e.g., to a beam in a room, and to some other object. It can be set at any angle.) The point at which the spool would come in contact with the ceiling should be well padded with some rather inelastic substance, in order that the spool may not rebound too severely. By throwing the spool along the rope a number of times daily, a man can acquire a powerful throw."

From the above quotations it will be obvious that we have many lessons to learn and adapt for ourselves from America, even while we need not agree with all that is maintained here. Thus the action of the throw may be better for certain individuals, certain places in the field, certain balls to be fielded, when the hand is kept at about the level of the shoulder (see the photograph of Hirst), or below that level. Murdoch, for instance, says, "When throwing, get into the way of never allowing your arm to get above the level of your shoulder: it must be a quick, wristy throw, and, with a little practice, you will get very accurate."

The captain should set a good example; he should also look out for keen fielders or keen practisers of fielding and try to turn these into respectable batsmen or bowlers, instead of starting with the latter and neglecting their fielding qualifications.

Among the best exercises for fielding is Fives. It trains the left hand and side, as well as the stooping-capacity. Boxing is another help, especially quick-foot boxing (which my friend Mr. F. V. Hornby has

XXXII.--Fielding a ground ball; no interval left for the ball to get through; body well down to the work.

[*Between pages 118 and 119.*

XXXIII.--A waiting position at point, where there is less foot-work than at most places. It is easier to rise quickly than to stoop quickly.

[*Between pages 118 and 119.*

XXXIV.--Preparing to throw in with the high action.

[*Between pages 118 and 119.*

described as "buzzing around") rather than the stiff-legged methodical slow kind. Boxing is fine for the "eye"--that is, for the co-operation of eye, foot, body, arm, etc. Diving is good for the wind; swimming for this and other purposes.

CHAPTER IV.

NOTES ON WICKET-KEEPING, CAPTAINING, IMPLEMENTS.

THESE subjects have been so thoughtfully dealt with in most of the well-known books on Cricket, that it will be unnecessary here to do more than sum up what seem to be the most useful points, and to add a few hints.

NOTES ON WICKET-KEEPING.

"The prevailing neglect of wicket-keeping is a gross folly. First as regards those who are to be regular wicket-keepers, why do they never practise? Their art is every whit as difficult as batting, and it is astonishing how its supreme importance to the efficiency of an eleven is overlooked. There is probably no hope of getting a really good man out on a good wicket, which can be compared to the chance of his sending a catch to the wicket-keeper before his eye is in. Sometimes these chances are missed, and no one notices anything.... Every member of any team would gain if he were taught how to keep wicket in early youth. In the first place it certainly helps the eye in batting. The problem of judging pace, pitch, and break is exactly the same in both cases. Next, it teaches sureness of hand in fielding. A field who has learnt wicket-keeping must find any catch, especially if it does not involve running, mere child's play compared with a chance behind the sticks. It is impossible that any such continuous exercise of hand and eye of the most subtle description could be anything but valuable to the general quickness and sureness both of fielding and batting. Lastly, even if all the eleven do not learn to keep wicket, there ought always to be one or more ready to take the place of the regular man, in case of injury or absence."--*Edward Lyttelton.*

In the plea for all-roundness we have already urged that every player should be able to keep wicket a little, or at any rate should practise with the ball and stump (see above). Wicket-keeping is useful not only for its own sake and for the sake of the place which it may bring in the team, but also as excellent discipline for short slip. The bowler himself must be able to take the ball when it is thrown in by the fielders--and it is generally thrown in remarkably badly--and to knock off the bails neatly and surely. The captain, when he is not a bowler, sees more of the game--

the strength or weakness of the bowling and so on--if he is at the wicket than if he is at point or elsewhere. As to fielding at mid-off, mid-on, and out in the country, even for these places wicket-keeping encourages quick bending and reaching, and general alertness of mind and unflagging attention--merits which should be but seldom are insisted on in what we may call the ordinary positions. The wicket-keeper must, in sheer self-defence, be quick not merely to move but also to anticipate; he must be accurate to time the ball and to use his wrist and fingers; he must adapt himself readily, as when a ball is badly sent in by cover; he must observe the bowler and--half unconsciously--the batsman; he must remember how this or that ball will break, and so on; he must indeed know the whole game--all this, let us repeat, if only in self-defence and to save trouble. In contrast to him, the deep-fielder may go to sleep, or "stug" himself on his heels with legs stiff and "thinking other things," without appreciable interest in each and every ball. The wicket-keeper dares not sleep: it would be as much as his face or fingers are worth.

The habit of watching each ball carefully, of being ever ready beforehand, is a habit that every batsman, every fielder and, we may add, every watcher requires. A personal interest is attached habitually to absolutely the whole performance and to each of the performers. The wicket-keeper, whether he be captain or not, takes a more than fatherly interest in every part of the play, for the sake of himself if not of his team.

Besides this, the almost compulsory pluck, since many balls, like nettles, hurt less if taken boldly, the balance-shifting, the stooping and stretching now here, now there, are certainly good for all play as well as for other games, for physical development, and for health (especially as a preventive for constipation). Anyone who studies the various positions (in photographs or in actual play) of Mr. McGregor, of Storer, of any expert, will realise the truth of this at once.

Nor is it possible, I think, even for a spectator to watch the game satisfactorily unless he has sometimes stood himself behind the sticks and seen the play from that point of view. The following hints may be of use to those who wish to try wicket-keeping.

Every writer advises the wicket-keeper who has taken a ball on the leg-side to put down the wicket on the chance of the batsman being out of his ground. This is a good rule, though it is by no means easy to take a ball on the leg-side, partly because the batsman himself obscures the view. This is one reason why Hirst suggests that for fast bowling the not over-good wicket-keeper should stand back unless the batsman often runs out.

To knock off the bails sharply on ordinary occasions is not so easy a task. It is necessary to be able to take any ball neatly in spite of the break and the bound. Hence it is good practice to get players to throw balls in to the wicket from various parts of the field. Such practice helps both wicket-keeper and fielders, but we never had it at school and of course at a college no one takes any trouble about fielding. The wicket-keeper can tell the fielder how and why his throwing is unsatisfactory, and can see that the other fielders back up properly.

The wicket-keeper should be the adviser of the captain, pointing out to him these details and also any useful changes of position. He may advise the bowlers as well--but with discretion, lest he be confounded. Captains and bowlers do not use their wicket-keeper nearly enough. He ought to be an invaluable guide-book.

Dr. W. G. Grace describes the wicket-keeper's position as follows:--

"Their hands are touching each other unless the ball is wide of the wicket, and catching or stumping is done without any show or fuss. They always stand with a full front to the bowler, and seldom move the feet unless the ball is very wide."

The wicket-keeper has to stretch in various directions with right or left hand, now up, now down, now straight out. He needs the power of stooping sideways. At the end of each extension, or at some intermediate place, he must be able to draw back his hand or hands slightly so that they "give" to the ball. If one studies the different places at which the ball is taken, one can soon devise exercises to make the movements of the legs and trunk and arms easier and quicker. The fast full movements are essential to success. Boxing would be among the best of trainings for this as for most athletic skill where large and--with many people--unwieldy limbs have to be moved rapidly in any one of numerous ways according as the quick eye shall telegraph to the obedient yet commanding brain.

NOTES ON CAPTAINING, ESPECIALLY AT SCHOOLS.

It often struck me, when I lectured to Civil Service candidates at Cambridge, that to captain a Cricket or Football team well was an infinitely better recommendation for a post than to know the dates of all the wars and battles of the Romans. The former is a test of something more than phonograph-accuracy. It is a test of leadership--of which virtue the crammed smug who can only just scrape through the riding examination may be quite devoid. But the art of captaincy counts nothing here: it only counts in character and life.

Besides the power to command others, the ideal captain must have all-round knowledge if he is to be able to find out where lie the strengths and weaknesses of his team; he should have some practical and personal acquaintance with all kinds of bowling and fielding as well as with wicket-keeping and batting, so that he may give timely advice.

There is no need to carry the instructing of a team to an American Football excess, but a hint from the land of exaggerations may be of use. The Captain frequently consults every possible authority. Before an important match--let us say between Harvard and Yale--old boys will come down and talk over the team and the tactics and arrange special "plays." Every Captain should have a Committee which he may consult when he is in doubt.

While he is choosing his team he should look among the juniors, as Mr. Lyttelton advises. If he is a School-captain, he may notice two or three boys keen on fielding and on practice generally (and, by the way, he himself should set a good example here); perhaps these boys are trying the stump-practice suggested in a previous chapter. Well, let him decide to turn these boys into batsmen and bowlers as well, by urging them to whatever helps he thinks good--perhaps to the practice with a bat along a line chalked on the floor and to other exercises suggested here. Anyhow he must always be looking out not only for promising young players, but also for keen young fielders. The desire for batting or bowling may be taken for granted. It is the fielders that are wanted. But of course the batting and bowling must be duly considered. There should be at least one left-handed bowler. And there should assuredly be an extra wicket-keep. Since the weather is so prominent a factor in the game, and as some players are almost hopeless on a difficult wicket, it might be suggested that the eleven for the most important matches should have a wider margin for choice than is usual, though the possible names must, for the sake of convenience, be decided on at least by the previous day. So much for the choice of the team; and now for its practice.

As the team need not be decided on finally, till as late as possible, so neither need be the positions of its members in the field, nor the order of going in. The positions and the order should be occasionally changed.

The captain should insist on punctuality, on neatness of clothing, perhaps even--if he dare--on clean hands as well as a pure heart, and certainly on keenness. At school he should try to get the most distinguished old boys to say a few words to the eleven.

He should also insist on all-roundness; he should insist that every member occasionally keep wicket, and (as we have said above) occasionally field in a place not his own, and occasionally bowl, and occasionally bat under difficulties--as with a broom-stick at stump-cricket or "snob." Nothing more quickly reveals the crooked bat. The captain himself should practise all these things, and especially fielding: otherwise what right has he to curse? If he sees the interest flagging, he should arrange more exciting matches. And he might do worse than devise some system of handicaps.

When the members of a visiting eleven have arrived, the captain's first thought must be for them: he must put himself in their place. He may delegate his duties to the second or third man in his team, so that he may attend to the details of the ground and the play.

Before and during a home or "foreign" match he must set an example of careful training and pure living, making it clear that excess is not manliness. He must not be a prig: he need not say, "Don't do that"; he can say, "I shouldn't do that if I were you." He is not a schoolmaster, and, even if he were, he might do worse than use that turn of phrase.

If he wins the toss, he should probably put his own side in. Many hold this to be a rule without exception. Anyhow, he should inspect the ground and notice any peculiarities of light, etc.

During the play he must be watchful of all sorts of things, and in the field he should therefore be as near to the wicket as possible. Point is a good place; wicket-keeping is still better, for then he can judge of the bowling and give hints to the bowlers. If he himself be a bowler he should have a candid friend who isn't one; this candid friend *must* be consulted.

Other hints are given in abundance by the many well-known writers on the game; to whose books we can safely refer the reader for such hints as that the fast bowler should be put on against the tail of the enemy; that the erratic bowler may be put on to break up a well-set pair.

These books the captain must read for himself. He must make notes from them, unless he has a superlative memory. He must think. He must observe. He must be tactful without weakness. Indeed, he should be far the most intelligent man in the eleven; and, if he is, he is probably worth his place in the eleven even if the utmost that he can do is to eat and drink in sensible moderation, and watch and field with unflagging energy.

NOTES ON IMPLEMENTS.

One of the ablest of writers on Cricket, Mr. W. J. Ford, suggests "what the cricket-bag should contain, apart from the actual weapons of offence and defence." He says: "It is a great addition to one's comfort to have spare socks and handkerchiefs (we may add vest and shirt) on board; a small bandage is often useful, especially adhesive bandage. If you are lumbagic or rheumatic, don't omit a cholera belt of red flannel, and do not forget to put it on when you come in steaming from a century, and have to sit in a draughty pavilion. Sticking-plaster is often useful, so is a hair-brush, likewise bags for boots; nothing is gained by mixing up muddy boots with flannels, sweater, and blazer. Add a button-hook and shoe-horn."

Boots are generally admitted to be preferable to shoes. They should be easy, but not too easy. The American pattern of boot is among the best, though anything more hideous than the black Lawn Tennis horror it would be impossible to conceive. The boots *must* be white. A high authority says that they need not have many nails, but too many nails are better than too few, lest one trip or slip when one turns. It is common sense, as Shrewsbury says, to put two near the toe, as runners do. Extra nails should be kept in the cricket-bag, with the means for inserting them. A good nail is the sparrowbill (from Shaw and Shrewsbury, Queen's Square, Nottingham), or the Nottingham nail.

Clothing in general, as Ranjitsinhji says, should satisfy the demands of "ease, convenience, and comfort, as well as of health and cleanliness. The shirt ought to be of canvas, wool, or flannel: flannel is always preferable if the wearer can put up with the irritation. Both trousers and shirt should be made to fit loosely, not flappingly. Boys are in the habit of putting on belts. This is a mistake, since the noise the belt makes may at times be mistaken for a catch at the wicket. I advise instead scarves or sashes, which also have a smarter appearance." So far as health is concerned, the flannel shirt (which is worn by most professionals) renders the wearer less liable to chill after a sweat, but hardens him far less than the linen shirt. Under either can be worn a vest, after the habit of Shrewsbury and others, if the weather is at all cold. The sash is not healthy, even though it is smarter than the belt--which, by the way, need not be at all noisy.

Clean flannels should be used as often as possible, since to wear things already rich in waste-products is not for the best. And flannels should never be kept in closed apartments. At Columbia University, in America, the lockers had wire trellis-work and not wooden covers, and the small changing room for hundreds of men was quite free from disagreeable smell.

In case of severe heat a light sun-hat is safe.

In case of cold weather a sweater is usual. To field well with cold hands is a miracle. At the beginning of the season thick kid gloves might be worn, as they are by Abel and Shrewsbury; or at least they can be made to cover those parts of the hand that blister most readily. Adhesive plaister round the finger will save friction if a blister has already formed and burst or been pricked.

The pads should be carefully chosen with a view to ease and lightness as well as protection. Shrewsbury's idea of an extra piece to protect the knee is to be commended. Otherwise let the pads be only just thick and heavy enough to give the feeling and the reality of safety. The fastenings should be good and not of inferior leather or elastic.

Here as elsewhere this advice holds good, to choose your implements for yourself; try before you buy; treat them with respect; learn how to mend them; carry about the means of mending them. A "housewife" with needles, good thread, scissors, safety pins, etc., will be invaluable. With a view to care and cleanliness, keep your best bat in some sort of a cover.

As to the bat, for men and full-sized boys its weight might be 241/2 to 25 oz., but that is less important than the ease with which the blade of the bat rises. For a very slow wicket an extra 11/2 to 2 oz. might be advisable, and hence at least two bats may be taken in the bag, if only in case of change of weather. But a comfortable feel is the great requisite, a comfortable feel not merely as you stand and hold the bat but also as you move and use the bat. If you have active feet and good shoulders and trunk then you may manage a heavier bat than if you have less active feet and a weaker forearm and wrist. The handle should bend lithely backwards and forwards rather than sideways. It can be made thicker by wash-leather if the hands are moist; and if they are wet, by the rubber covering, which adds over an ounce of weight to the bat and thus helps the blade to rise. The wood of the bat is often found to be cut away from all the bat except just the part with which one *hopes* to stroke the ball. This, as Shrewsbury says, is not desirable, since one cannot always judge the rise of the ball absolutely, and though a stroke with the extra-fat part of the blade may be "very, very nice," the stroke with the thin part may be "horrid." Shrewsbury's bats are less exaggerated, so that they allow the batsman more surface to drive well with.

The blade should be oiled say once a fortnight, but not too heavily, lest the driving power be decreased. One needs a nice soft bat which after use shall show not cracks but dents--a bat which shall have a slightly hollowed middle-blade. In its infancy, use it with soft old balls by preference; train it gently as a boxer might train his face to receive hard blows. Notice where the dents come, and correct your play accordingly; those which are off the best driving part are like the blue marks of the schoolmaster's pencil. When the bat is injured, use string-binding in preference to pegs; learn how to do that string-binding, and keep a little string in your bag.

In your bag keep also a comfortable pair of batting-gloves and a ball. "Neither a borrower nor a lender be"; certainly never lend a ball. I would add also a Lawn Tennis ball and a stick; the latter if only in case of a walk in new country, the former in case of a wet day when Snob-cricket is far better than loafing. Every pavilion should allow of this game, as every ship should allow of deck Cricket. The game should be played with a soft ball and stick or stump, not with a hard ball and bat.

If you take a favourite book also, a Membook or Diary with a pencil, and also a complete list of all the things you want in the bag, so that you never have to borrow what may not fit you, or be as the foolish virgins, you will be better off than nine out of ten cricketers are.

CHAPTER V.

THE IMPORTANCE OF ALL-ROUNDNESS IN CRICKET.

"THE right and proper thing would be for cricketers to pay equal attention to bowling, batting, and fielding, especially in their young days. All are equally essential parts of the game. Why not regard them as equally valuable? The doctrine of the division of labour holds good in cricket as elsewhere, but every cricketer should, as far as lies in him, qualify himself for every emergency. Most amateurs take no trouble whatever with their bowling, except in matches."--RANJITSINHJI.

I have heard it said that Richter, the great conductor, could himself play every instrument used in his own orchestra, so that at once he knew where and how the general effect was weak. On the same principle the captain of a team should as a rule be an all-round player--a batsman, bowler, fielder, watcher--though there are some captains who do not excel much in any sphere except captaining, and yet are worth their place in their team.

But it is not merely the captain who gains by being an all-round player. Cricket has as its object to fit every cricketer for his all-round life, as games and exercises prepare young animals for their narrower life. We have used games with this result if not with this object for generations past; year by year, whether we know it or not, we shall have to rely on them more and more. And anyhow a certain time, perhaps amounting to hundreds of hours, is sure to be given to the play. Therefore it is as well to get the most that we can out of that time, and to get the most that we can out of each department of Cricket; in the spirit of Shrewsbury, studying it as a pleasant art; with Abel, entering into it keenly and smartly; and, like Hirst, aiming at many-sided excellence.

We cannot all be Hirsts, F. S. Jacksons, J. R. Masons, T. Haywards, A. G. Steels, and so on; that is obvious. But most players are content never to try, or else to try wrongly and then give up. There never was a greater error.

Let us consider batting alone. Even for successful and therefore enjoyable batting (batting has been, is, and will be most enjoyed and most sought after, and therefore has been, is, and will be least uncultivated; many cultivate nothing besides), even for this we need more than practice at a net or in a game, indispensable as these are in their proper place.

First of all, unless we are genius-players, we need a knowledge of bowling; we need not only to see the bowler's wrist and fingers, but also to get an idea of what will happen to the ball when it has left the fingers. In Tennis I never knew what was going to happen to a service until I learnt how to serve. Otherwise I played as if there would be no special cut or twist or drag. So practice in bowling may give the best knowledge of bowling for the batsman's purpose. Take a Lawn Tennis ball, and study the ways of producing various breaks, etc.--I recommend a Lawn Tennis ball because it shows the break more clearly, and can be used in a room; then produce these breaks with a Cricket ball (don't let it loose) before a large mirror. After a time you will know what to expect when you see certain signs, such as the middle and third finger curled inwards against the bowler's palm. Besides, when you have yourself bowled certain balls, you will know where the batsman generally hits them, and what faults he generally makes. You can avoid these faults, while on the other hand you can see at once, when you go in, where the fielding offers a gap. It is not every bowler who knows his own weak spots.

As a wicket-keeper one might learn still more about batting than one could as a bowler. It is amazing to me that so few wicket-keepers can bat even with moderate success. They seem to degenerate, like the idle watchers, with too much watching and too much "knowledge!" The wicket-keeper sees most of the game, and especially the batsman's faults and the bowler's merits of break, spin, change of pace, and so on. He has to watch the bowler's wrist and fingers. He should know precisely what balls should be left alone.

Only a few degrees less useful for batting is a knowledge of fielding in all parts of the field, though every fielder should have one or two specialities. The good fielder, when he bats, can remember the curl of the ball hit to third man; he can observe cover-point's attitude of slackness and steal an easy run, for he knows that a sloucher cannot run him out.

And to watch a game well--that may be as valuable a help for batting as bowling, wicket-keeping, or fielding. Shrewsbury will observe the play and its many niceties--the duel between a good bowler and a good batsman--from various parts of the field as he walks about; he will study length, pace, curl, the batsman's weakness. Some watchers appear to see *all* the faults. They don't play, but they may be made very useful as teachers, even if they only teach how to watch. One should watch the game not only as a whole, but also player by player; and in a single player one should observe the bat alone, whether it be straight or not; the left foot; the left elbow; the right leg; and the results on play.

All-roundness is thus nearly a necessity for full success in batting, unless one is a genius-player. It is quite a necessity for full enjoyment. It is also a duty towards the team. But, besides its effects on batting, it has still more obvious effects on bowling and fielding themselves.

Bowling should be tried and practised by every member of the team, for the sake of the team as well as of the self. It is a pleasure to the bowler, if it be well done. Were proof needed, why else do so many captains so often put themselves on to bowl? Perhaps it may be a smaller pleasure than batting, somewhat as to besiege an enemy may be a smaller pleasure than to resist the siege or to make a sally. But bowling allows more errors--a single bad ball, unlike a single error in batting, need not be the end of the performance. Anyhow, bowling is a pleasant change from fielding, and gives one an extra chance of playing for a team. And, unless one plays for a team, Cricket is not much sport! A fair bowler is becoming more and more useful to his side every year, with these billiard-table wickets.

Wicket-keeping offers a similar inducement. At the last moment Jones fails--he hurts his thumb--why shouldn't he? "Well," says the captain, "Smith (that's you) can keep wicket a bit." You are now, for the time, in the team.

The same will apply to fielding also. To take an extreme case, an inferior field has to be terribly superior with the bat or ball or both if he wants to get a place in a Yorkshire or Australian eleven. For his own sake, as well as for the sake of his side, a boy or man must be safe and smart in the field. The work is often dull--six overs without any ball, but one can watch the bat and study where the man is weak. Or one can imagine oneself as the fielder to whom the ball is hit. In case this shall appeal to you, patient alertness and long waiting to pounce on an opportunity, are makers of character, as General Grant proved, and of money, as the army of American financiers show weekly. Fielding is worth doing well, and therefore worth practising well, whether with an india-rubber ball against a wall (for stopping and for catching), or with any ball and a stump or stick. Let two players, as we have suggested, stand on opposite sides of it, and throw in at it, varying the distance, and occasionally sending catches instead. A third player can act as a wicket-keeper or as a bowler receiving the throw-in. If I were a captain I should encourage this kind of thing; I should look about for smart fields, and get them to practise in this and other ways. I should also get them to bowl a bit. I should not always pick out the batsmen and bowlers first, and neglect the fielders. A Vernon Royle, a Lohmann, a Gunn are worth a place in a team apart from other merits. They save runs not only by catching, not only by backing up, not only by stopping hits, not only by running in, but by their reputation--the batsmen simply dared not run a short one when Royle was at cover--and by their contagious influence.

I think that all-roundness justifies itself, and therefore all-round practice justifies itself, even from the point of view of the selfish batsman who wants the best possible innings, quite apart from one's increased enjoyment as a change bowler, perhaps as a wicket-keeper, certainly as a fielder, and no less certainly as a watcher.

But how? What is the secret of all-roundness? This book will offer advice to many, and hope to not a few. If you have not yet paid attention to the very foundations, the very A B C of good play (especially of batting and fielding), such as the positions and movements of the feet, the full extensions of the limbs, the body-swing, the balance and prompt recovery, then you need not yet despair. Practice in these things will be far from useless for general athletic fitness; there is scarcely a game but absolutely involves them.

This, after all, is my chief plea for all-roundness: not merely that probably much time *will* be given to Cricket anyhow, and that the player may as well learn the whole of Cricket; not only that thus his play will be pleasanter (or less dull), more useful to his health and physical development, more useful to his side, more useful to Cricket itself, but also that he will be better prepared for other games and other occupations, no matter what they are or shall be. He is a handy man, a footy and leggy man (if the ugly words may be pardoned, because they mean much), a ready man, disciplined and patient, yet alert and quick here and anywhere.

If you are going to play Cricket at all, or even to watch Cricket at all, all-roundness is worth while. Otherwise your days of fielding or of watching will be for the most part wasted; your minutes of batting will not grow into quarter-hours, half-hours, hours; your bowling will never have even a minute at all. Be a specialist if you like, but don't be only a specialist. Try if you cannot do the other things at least moderately well.

Within the dominion of batting also there is need for all-roundness. Mr. C. B. Fry aptly remarks:--"The great defect of school coaching is that boys are taught to play forward and nothing else. Boys are not taught to play back or to use their feet properly, either in turning to place the ball or in running out to drive; nor are they taught to alter their play according to the state of the wicket."

He himself is an all-round batsman. So is W. G.; as one of his innumerable admirers says:--"What W. G. did was to unite in his mighty self all the good points of all the good players, and to make utility the criterion of style. He founded the modern theory of batting by making forward and back play of equal importance, relying neither on the one nor the other, but on both."

All-roundness is of value to every player--all-roundness in Cricket generally; all-roundness in the special departments of batting, and of fielding; to be able merely to catch well, or merely to stop well, or merely to run well, or merely to throw in well, must not content the player.

CHAPTER VI.

FAULTS IN PLAY AND PRACTICE.

NO part of this book do I edit with such confidence as the part that deals with faults. I seem to have had every one of a certain class, though not want of endurance and strength, nor a bad eye, nor unwillingness; ignorance I had, not apathy. My chief sin--of which I shall speak below--was that I tried to practise the whole rather than its parts; I had matches, games, nets in abundance, and a few fielding lessons, but made hardly any progress.

And so it is with most. They try the whole--or at least the whole stroke--all together at first, seldom if ever concentrating their attention on any one part. They do what is natural, and this is usually "wrong." They have no method of learning, except repetition which will only increase and ingrain the faults. Authorities recommend net-practice; but much of it is surely next to useless until the A B C has been mastered by batsman and bowler. If there are three bowlers at a net, the batsman gets excessive variety of bowling, the balls follow one another in too quick succession, each dulling the memory of the previous two; after the stroke--in which there is little incentive for carefulness--the batsman does not recover balance and prepare to run; the bowler has small inducement to lead up to a special head-ball, as he would by a consecutive series in a game, and, besides, he gets the wrong intervals--not a series, then a rest, but a single ball, then a rest; last, and not least, there are few fielders.

Let us be more concrete, and point out a few of the definite faults which are encouraged rather than removed by ordinary net play and games.

Stand directly behind the wicket in a school or college game, or behind a practice-net, and watch the batsman play forward; you will generally see the bat move up and back and then towards the ball in a far from straight line. That fault, it is well known, may be partially remedied by practice along a chalk line on the bed room or pavilion floor. "Play with a straight bat," is the most familiar commandment. Besides, you may notice that his left foot does not go out nearly to the full extent of which a young and vigorous limb should be capable, and it does not go out straight; the bat may move towards the ball, but between it and the left foot is a great gap, through which the ball may pass. This is not the only fatal result. The left foot is sending the weight of the body too much to the left, to the leg-side, instead of straight down upon the ball: there is loss of power. Now does the fault lie with the hands and arms and shoulders that move and direct the bat, or with the left leg and foot? Sometimes with both, but nearly always with the left leg and foot, which tend to get away from their work. The lesson is obvious; but I have never heard any coach advise players to practise their feet alone. Yet how else can one learn to control them--that is, if one does not control them instinctively--except by concentrating the mind on them *at first* and until they will of themselves do what one wants? Mr. C. B. Fry alone seems to realise the importance of the feet--of their correct positions and movements. For years I have been studying them in Racquets and Tennis, for years I have been convinced that this is why, *ceteris paribus*, most unsuccessful players are unsuccessful; for years I have been training mine; and at length, instead of being always unready and out of position in my racket-games, as I was at Marlborough, I am now told that I am almost invariably ready and in position. If this practice be vitally indispensable at Racquets and at Tennis, if it has proved abundantly worth while, why not at Cricket also? In what essential respects do strokes at Cricket differ herein from strokes at these games?

This is just one example of the lines on which much of the book is written. As, for my own games, I studied Latham and Standing, Brown and Pettitt, Fennell and Harradine, Saunders and Fairs, so here I have studied Abel, Hirst, and Shrewsbury. What they do regularly, if unconsciously, this I have found out by questions and by the incontrovertible evidence of photographs, and this I have then analysed and described especially for the benefit of beginners, but also, it is hoped, for the benefit of others who--like myself at my own games--played and played and played, practised and practised and practised, but wrongly, for want of simple teaching, for want of elementary apprenticeship, for want of knowledge and mastery of the very alphabet of play; and so scarcely improved but rather confirmed their bad habits.

Let me diverge for a moment to give a word of warning. To all such players--whether their form of exercise be Cricket or Racquets or Tennis or Lawn Tennis or other games--I would say: "Do not grudge time and trouble spent over the simple A B C, *at the start*; get over the drudgery; make the letters and words automatic--integral parts of your very self and of its cells, fibres, nerves, and muscles; then and not till then play naturally. But do not imagine that it is worth while to play naturally so long as at least one-third of the mechanism of your body is wrongly employed or else atrophied through neglect. Develop all your important muscles (for pray tell me what important muscles are not wanted by a good batsman, a good bowler, a good fielder), by prompt fast and full movements of the two sides of the body independently--a most vital point; by extension movements; by practice in weight-shifting and balance; by imitation-batting and its various motions, imitation-bowling, imitation-fielding and throwing, in a bedroom or elsewhere. (I do a little nearly every morning.) Then and not till then will you have a right to tell me that you can't play or can't improve in spite of nets and games. Then and not till then will I believe you. Till then, I repeat, you are not yet a real failure. You have not done yourself justice." For we wish in this book to prove several things that may give hope especially to young players and duffers, and to those who, alas, have abandoned our great national game in despair, because they have not found it worth the expenditure of money, time, tediousness, and disappointment.

Let us consider in how many respects one may very likely be making serious mistakes. Let us realise the multitude of possible faults.

1. First of all--as the photographs will clearly show, thanks to the new idea of the white line out from the middle stump--the feet are the foundations of successful and therefore of enjoyable play. Abel plays with his feet. We must have their positions and movements not only correct but also automatically correct--already integral parts of ourselves--if we would wait well, play forward well, play back well, pull well, drive well, step or jump out well, cut well, cut-drive well, bowl well, field well. So long as we have to be thinking consciously of our feet, we cannot focus our attention on the bowler's wrist or the batsman's bat. He who would succeed must--unless he be a genius, a born player--drill his feet for a few minutes almost every day. Such drill will be useful for many games and forms of sport, as for Football, Hockey, Track-athletics, self-defence, to say nothing of the mental and moral training which are indissolubly bound up with the physical.

2. Secondly, the weight and the balance of the body must be under control both during and after the stroke or other movement. Over his foot-work and equilibrium the keen fencer will spend many months; why should not the keen cricketer thus spend several hours? Does he not think that Cricket is of more value than many fencings? Now although the whole weight of the body must move together, especially in the forward stroke, yet perfect balance implies perfect (conscious or else sub-conscious) control of *all* the muscles, in Cricket scarcely to a less degree than in skating. To put the total force into batting or bowling would mean with the average player either a fall or a strain. But with special

practice the power is acquired. Almost any one can by sheer practice, even of the least scientific kind, learn to direct his limbs and yet maintain his balance in skating; and if in skating why not in Cricket also, particularly should special practice-exercises be devised? These have been devised, and are offered in this volume.

3. It is above all in the full extensions that average cricketers are weak. "I say, reach out and field them," is the complaint of the school captain; "Come forward to it; get your bat well over the ball--get right to the pitch of it," is the refrain of the coach. But if the ordinary person followed out the instructions he would perhaps tumble over. Extension of legs, trunk, arms--this can be mastered by proper practice. Fencers and boxers can master it; why not cricketers also?

4. Boxers and "Bartitsu" experts have to be alert on the balls of their feet, and ready to move now here, now there--not ever to lose poise, but to put the full weight, to make the full extension, to shoot out the required limb or limbs fast and straight and true. The batsman, the fielder, the bowler (at least after he has bowled), all have to be prompt commanders of their many-portioned persons, waiting for the unknown, or, rather, for some one out of the several knowns. At present we have scarcely any means, except the imagination, of practising preparedness for the unforeseen. But at least we can, again by specially contrived exercises as distinct from dumb-bells, weight-lifting, strain-exercisers, gymnastics, develop an almost incredible looseness of joint and litheness of limb, so that after a little play at the game itself, merely to have seen the ball will mean to have formed "the ready" in a moment, and to be waiting *in* "the ready"--"the ready" being that position from which the strokes, etc., are most easily and safely made; whereas without such practice we should have stood and waited in "the unready" and should either have missed the strokes, etc., altogether, or should have made them with difficulty and with risk.

5. Nor is it mere quickness to prepare that the cricketer needs; he needs also quickness to perform, to carry through. In the hundred yards sprint, one should not only start rapidly, one should also run rapidly. As training for this we require fast full movements, simple to begin with (first for the right side, then for the left); but afterwards more and more varied, complex, and speedy. Nothing could be better here than the Macdonald Smith system. Slow movements of strain are not to be recommended for Cricket purposes, except in so far as they strengthen the fingers and the wrist and the forearm. And even these parts should

not be strengthened till they have already become prompt to start and to move, lithe and supple under the control of the will.

6. A high authority, quoted in a previous chapter, asserts that Cricket does not need very special training. But we insist that, if one wishes--and one ought to wish--to run fast and vigorously and to move fast and vigorously (whether as a batsman or as a bowler or as a fielder), one should be in condition analogous to that of a football three-quarters. Quite apart from control of special muscles or sets of muscles, one must be able to run and move not only fast, but often; one must have endurance, or else one will amble after a ball--a disgusting sight to the true sportsman--instead of racing after it. And one should be calm; calmness, I find in my own case, is an inseparable accompaniment of good condition. Bad condition is a very serious fault; it "flusters" the player.

There is no space to enlarge upon errors in detail; for example, to warn the batsman against bending his right knee (except for the late cut), or against lifting his bat up and back in a crooked line before the stroke (this he can test by means of a looking-glass), or against standing too far from his work as if he were playing Lawn Tennis or Golf. These and other hindrances to success will be dealt with in the special chapters. Here let us rather try once again to emphasise *the* fault of faults.

"Don't slog at a ball well up to the off," "Don't pull"--these are not fundamental rules; they are good for nearly all beginners, but less applicable to him who has mastered the mechanism and elements of play already. *The* mistake is to have failed to master this mechanism; to have neglected the apprenticeship--an apprenticeship for a game which then becomes in itself an admirable apprenticeship for serious life as well as a relief from that life, and yet is both complex and to a great extent against nature in general and the nature of a player of ball-games in particular. To play forward with full force and with the bat near to the left foot and not tilted upwards--this implies a very special skill, with considerable restraint. The average player fails here. He has neglected to practise with concentration and care certain all-important parts of his forward-playing apparatus. He might have mastered each one of these parts and made it his own, and then have combined them; the straight full lunge with the weight thrown on to the left leg and with the right leg stretched straight; the complete forward-extension of the left elbow with some shoulder-movement; the turning of the left hand so that its knuckles shall face the bowler. For a late cut he might repeat, till they become easier and easier, the step across (an imaginary) wicket with the right foot, the shoulder-jerk, the forearm-jerk, the wrist-flick. Other strokes need other things; the pull needs the body-twisting from the hips; bowling needs not only large movements but also fine turns of the fingers and wrist. Let any player have neglected such mechanisms, and he need not wonder at ill-success. Should he disbelieve me, then he must watch some expert at work: if the expert will give an exhibition stripped, so much the better. This will certainly convince any one that the co-operation and co-ordination of many members of the body is demanded by nearly every department of the play.

The use of the left-side will then emerge clearly into its prominent importance. Cricket can claim infinitely more left-sided skill and power than any authority seems to imagine. A man is said to bat right-handed; but watch his ordinary play forward, feel his left shoulder and forearm and his left thigh: the stroke is only more right-sided than left-sided. In the drive along the ground, the left arm may serve as a powerful check, as it may in the late cut. Good fielding requires frequent quick and complete extensions of the left arm with power to catch while the extension is still complete. To throw in with the left hand nearly as well as with the right is an art alien to nearly every one; but alien by neglect and not by want of birthright. Every boy should be taught to throw with his left hand, or at least to pick up neatly with it. Nor need any one, until he has tried fairly and failed, despair of some success as a left-hand change-bowler, thanks to the break from the leg and the unfamiliar point of departure from round the wicket.

The utter inability of at least nine individuals out of ten to make a fast, full, and free extension with the arm in any unexpected direction is closely connected with their inability to throw the body's weight rapidly hither and thither without loss of balance, without sacrifice of "the ready."

Hence and from other sources arise many special failings, which the use of ordinary strain-apparatus or heavy dumb-bells would probably do very little to correct. He whose *first* aim has been to become strong--a lifter or puller or pusher--may have hampered his rapidity of movement for years, if not for all his active years. Of course he needs *some* strength to hold and control a bat; but even that should not be developed until the limbs already have their promptitude and speed. It is not a matter of physical "development"--a term used by ignoramuses to veil a multitude of faulty methods. It is a matter of *proper* physical development, one tending to *freedom*. And against this freedom I am sure that the use of "manly" implements and conditions by boys must militate. Most of the highest authorities are agreed here; I select one or two quotations:--

"There are three great difficulties with which young boys have to cope--the regulation size of the ball, the full distance between the wickets, and the full size of the bat. Some attempt has been made to provide them with bats to suit them, but, unfortunately, most small-sized bats are made of inferior wood and are badly shaped. All implements and conditions of the game should in every case be proportioned to the players."

"Why in the world is it that small boys are made to play cricket with the same sized ball as Dr. Grace and Mr. Bonnor use? What a ludicrous piece of mischievous uniformity this is! The only hope of making cricket as really attractive and useful to young boys as it might be, is to reduce the size of the ball as well as the size of the bat, and keep the full distance. At present a diminutive brat pummels the big ball with all his might, and it barely reaches cover point; his best half-volley drive goes meekly into mid-on's hands--or, rather, it would, if the ball were not too big to get there. Not only is his hitting spoilt: the throwing becomes painful, and the bowling in spite of the short distance strains the shoulder. The game is out of proportion because the fields need never occupy their proper place, and the ball never travels to them as it will hereafter, nor can they be expected to stop it clean when it does reach them. The fact must be insisted on, that it is all important to make cricket thoroughly attractive to young players, or they will probably give it up."

"Small boys cannot obviously use full-sized bats. The mischief that results if they do is fatal. It is impossible for them to play straight, because the end of the bat smites the ground and the stroke comes to naught. Besides which, the excessive weight makes them late for all the hits."

Another disadvantage of this premature use of heavy implements is that it encourages tension. Players like Mr. L. C. H. Palairet are singularly free from it; but they are so by nature. With comparatively few exceptions, the habit of tension is, alas, almost national. We English are a stiff-bodied and stiff-legged people: the legs and body may be fairly big and muscular, but the muscles are of the wrong order for Cricket--akin to lumps of wood rather than to lithe pieces of snake. Even when we watch cricket we often watch it with tense and strained bodies: we do not sit reasonably comfortable.

Owing to these and other faults hundreds give up the game. They say that they can not play it regularly (because it takes up too much time), and that they do not play it well enough for it to be worth while. They may be anxious to keep in practice and to improve, but they do not know how.

Others are not at all anxious; theirs is the most serious hindrance of all--they are not keen. This is to some extent what is called "constitutional," but is largely due to ignorance of the ways of learning, and to neglect of some one or more of the branches of play. As to-day a person may be a clergyman or a surgeon or a physician, but is seldom a healer of the whole patient, so in Cricket a person will be a batsman or a bowler without any noticeable ambition to enlarge his sphere of skill. In batting he may even be a fast-wicket batsman, failing regularly on caked wickets. For fielding he has no enthusiasm; or, if he is a fielder, he is perhaps good either at catching or at picking up or at throwing in--not at all.

Lack of enthusiasm, lack of concentration on and absorption in every part of the play as its turn comes round, this is almost fatal if not to success at least to success that is worth having. And I am not sure that the grievous and fatal error of allowing the eye to leave the ball too soon may not be to some extent a result of incomplete concentration.

CHAPTER VII.

GENERAL TRAINING FOR CRICKET.

THERE are some who deny that any special or even general training is needed for Cricket. Ranjitsinhji says that "cricket does not demand that severe course of training which is required by such athletic pursuits as football and running." That it does not *get* that severe course is obvious; what it demands, let us examine in the light of a few facts which no one would dream of disputing.

If the game is to flourish, if it is to remain interesting (or, shall we say, to become interesting again), our modern plumb wickets demand many more and far better bowlers, especially fast and medium bowlers. We hear laments over the brief career of a Richardson as if it were inevitable; but knowing the nature of stimulants--they are a kind of whip or spur--and that meat is one kind, tea and coffee another, alcohol another, to say nothing of the irritant stimulants such as pepper, mustard, and salt, can we expect a man to go unharmed through a series of hard seasons if he uses the whip or the spur even "in moderation" twice or three times daily during many years? Now has any well-known fast bowler ever yet paid any real and special attention to diet (apart from the general adherance to "moderation" in quantity)? Has any, besides, kept up quick and interesting exercise of his body during the idle months? I do not allude to weight-lifting, which may be fatal to fast bowling, but to sensible exercises and breathing-exercises, say for ten minutes each morning. To me it seems obvious that a fast bowler, if he wishes to keep up his pace and endurance, must keep up at least as severe a course as football or running require.

Secondly, if the game is to be interesting and to flourish, we need good fielders--the second and I think the most important reform to counteract successful batting. We need fielders to be energetic, always ready to stretch out in any direction, to run in any direction at full pace, alert to back up, quick to throw in accurately. Yet how many dozen fielders outside the Yorkshire and Australian teams, how many out of our thousands, are even reasonably brisk, especially at the end or even in the middle of a day in the country? For my own part I should like to see a very severe course of training here; if the boys or men are going to stand there at all, let them at any rate stand in "the ready." The listless loafing in most school and college matches is positively disgusting.

Thirdly, the batsman as well as the bowler and fielders should "feel the nip," as Abel and Hirst and Shrewsbury agree; it is the result of fitness, and expresses itself chiefly in the fingers and wrist (at my games I get it in the balls of my feet also). The player should feel it not only during the first few minutes of play, but to some extent up to half-time at any rate. Mere endurance is not enough--this is not what I mean. I mean that joy in having hands and feet, which should be a general condition, but actually is an occasional condition--how many of the players can tell you why they have it at such-and-such a time? I find it comes naturally from my training, which is as severe as I should adopt for football or athletics, yet is a "training without straining," a training that need not interfere with brain-work.

It is more than endurance, this feeling; it is enduring freshness. And, until both bowlers and fielders get it somehow or other, Cricket will probably be a one-sided affair--poor sport for the majority. It is as helps towards this enduring freshness that I offer a few hints as worth putting into practice. Let their results speak for them or against them.

Many professionals rely on walking, with an occasional run, as their sole exercise, and "not too much" as their sole law about diet, alcohol, and tobacco. Abel may practice a few strokes in a room; Hirst may play Knur-spell; Shrewsbury may get some practice on cokernut matting. But for the most part net-practice and Cricket itself are waited for and relied on. Now all these things are good, but by themselves are not good enough for ordinary people.

One notices a bowler run slackly after a ball, lest he should find himself out of breath. Breathing exercises are needed by nine cricketers out of ten. The whole apparatus--low and middle and upper--should be developed by full and frequent inhaling through the nose, by brisk movements, by diving and swimming, and so on. He who has a bad wind, whether because some parts of the breathing apparatus are undeveloped or overdeveloped, or owing to fatness, indigestion, constipation, smoking, drinking, deficient sleep, or sleep in bad air, muscular tension, etc., is at a most serious disadvantage. Either he does not run and move with speed, and thus is to that extent an inferior batsman, bowler, or field, or else he does move and becomes "puffed," and of necessity loses "eye" and nerve. As Murdoch remarks:--"There is no doubt in my mind that running affects your eyesight in a greater or lesser degree, according to the condition you are in."

The following quotation is also sound common sense:--"The better your condition, the less chance there is of your doing what boxers have generally to do, and what I have often heard batsmen express as sparring for wind. If you should care to go in for a system of training, it can only do good; for in every department of the game, the better condition you are in, the better chances you have of doing yourself justice. Good condition means stamina, and you certainly want this to play a long innings; and solely for the want of it I have seen batsmen get out. You certainly require it, should you have a day's outing in the field, especially so if you are a bowler; so my advice is to make it a rule to be as fit as possible."

But to return to breathing, breathing slowly outwards, together with a relaxing of the muscles, tends not only to endurance (by economy of force), but also to calmness, patience, and contentment. All players, and especially the nervous, need a very fine course of nerve-training in these.

With the calmness, however, there must be promptness and quickness. The senses must send a quick message to the brain, which must then give a quick order to the muscles, which in their turn must quickly work together in harmony. As to the senses, we need to have a clear eye, and--a much under-estimated help--a keen ear. Therefore we need clear blood, which will give us also clean joints and clean limbs--joints free from deposits, limbs free from excessive fat or water or waste. We need a brisk intellect, including a sensitive observation and retentive memory. These may all be trained by the Macdonald Smith System, which I should like to see as a part of national education. It is not complete, but it is extremely useful. It will help, for example, to give a quick and fairly strong wrist without that stiffness which is singularly fatal in nearly every province of the game.

Exercises according to this system, together with exercises in complete extensions, will be suggested in other chapters. I should like to do away altogether with that popular test "How large does the muscle look?" and to substitute for it, among other tests, "How far does the limb stretch?" In the other chapters will also be emphasised the importance of balance: one must be able to use weight without loss of poise.

The subject of training has been dealt with in a special volume of this library, and food in particular has formed the subject of "Muscle, Brain, and Diet." Here we must be content to select a very few hints of a general kind. Let us begin with food.

To what we shall say there will be exceptions. Some players are at their very best after the grossest excesses, perhaps partly because the blood has been cleared for the time by the quantities of stimulants; but such excesses cannot be relied on to produce the very best. Moreover, few such men last long, even though for a while the outward eye sees little or no decay. If any one thinks he must have an occasional "bust," let it be very occasional. Far safer advice would be as follows:--Find out what is nourishing to you. Don't assume that it must be meat. It may be cheese or Plasmon, or the pulses or nut foods or good grain-foods, all of which have plenty of blood-forming and cell-building proteid, as this little table will show:--

APPROXIMATE AMOUNT OF PROTEID IN VARIOUS FOODS (UNCOOKED).

Beef 20.

Fish 10.

Eggs 12 to 16.

Cheese 20 to 30.

Plasmon 70 to 80.

Peas (dried) 21.

Lentils and haricots 23.

Nuts 10 to 24 (walnuts and filberts 14).

Hovis 10.

Wheat and whole-wheat products 11.

Roots and tubers, vegetables and salads, and most fruits, though useful for other purposes, are poor in proteid.

Take enough nourishment: let that be your first rule. Take say four to five ounces of proteid a day, trying and testing several sources when you have little at stake (as on Sundays). You can generally control one of your daily meals. Start the experiment there. Eat slowly and enjoy the taste fully. Don't swallow disagreeable masses of vegetables or slops: that is neither sense nor science. On Sunday give the in-side a holiday: that is both sense and religion. Let the Sabbath rest for the digestion be your second rule.

Find out what are stimulants and narcotics, and let your third rule be this: never to become the slave of them; never to rely on them; above all, never to let yourself increase the quantity so that you have to add to the previous dose before anything "begins to count." This is a practical counsel, rather than a counsel of perfection.

If you are against any great change, any experimentation, then let me give you some commonplaces, they are better than nothing. Keep to moderation in quantity; go early to bed, till you find the fascinations of a fresh head and body in the morning and throughout the day and many days to follow, greater than the fascination night after night of drinking, smoking, and cards; sleep with shut mouth, open windows, light clothes;

rise or work early; clean yourself with warm water and friction; invigorate yourself with cool or cold water and friction, then with brisk full movements; relax your limbs for a few moments now and at bed-time; never have anxiety about anything; never have ill-feeling against anyone; add to this little repertoire all helps that are available everywhere, however poor you may be--not champagne, but air-and-light baths, massage, and so on. Be clean with mind and mouth as well as in body and limb; keep your physical vigour for play; study health, not morbidly, but sensibly; be able to box, and supplement Cricket with other games and exercises.

During the play, play with your whole heart and soul, as a member of a team, but as an important and special member. Concentrate not only while batting, bowling, and fielding, but while watching the niceties and learning new points, and also while practising at a net or in a room; as when you exercise yourself at starting in various directions, or at step-dancing (as Mr. C. B. Fry advises), or at fast extensions, such as stooping, or at throwing movements, or at bowling-movements. Concentrate as if there were nothing else at all in the whole world but to do each of these things very well--to do each of them better than any one ever expected you would be able to. Throw your nerve-power, your will and mind, your self, into your muscles, or, if you prefer, into their reflection in the looking-glass. Each pavilion should have a large mirror in it. At odd moments imagine different movements, different strokes--and especially when undesirable thoughts come, unless you have strength of mind to tire yourself out before sleep.

Perhaps you will never become very great at batting, though fair batting seems to me to be within the reach of most people who take the proper trouble; perhaps not very great at bowling either, though how most boys or men should expect to bowl while they have huge muscle-areas and tiny muscle areas so ill-controlled, I cannot tell; at least, however, you may become great at fielding--quick to start and run, sure to catch. Think what that needs--and practise accordingly.

So much for the attention when you are playing, practising, or training, and when you are idle or inclined to worse than idleness. Insist on complete concentration; recall again and again your wandering thought, your roving eye and inquisitive ear. Say to yourself, "This one thing I do now with all my heart."

But apply that same concentration to whatever you do, if it is really worth doing, or has to be done. Let each thing in turn be the sole thing for which you were born. When other things are to be done, resolve not to do or think Cricket. I believe that this may prove an excellent cure for staleness.

The question of "staleness" has already been well discussed by Mr. A. G. Steel, Mr. Edward Lyttelton, and many others. In my own games I believe I am never stale now, and I attribute this blessing chiefly to my diet. In the "trinity of games," Cricket, there need be no staleness through boredom, if only the player will cultivate all-roundness of play, and will prepare for and supplement his Cricket by good brain-work, simple exercises, and general health-culture. Much staleness is the result of excessive, or else badly-chosen, or else badly-used, or else deficient exercise, food, air, and so on; some is the result of the law of vitality and of victory, that energy and success shall not be level, but shall have tides; scarcely any, I believe, rests with Cricket itself. As more than one able writer has pointed out, a successful cricketer is, *ipso facto*, *not* stale.

I am reluctant to preach, but it is useless to edit a book on cricket without making clear to the reader that there is a problem for him to solve *for himself*. No one else can possibly solve it for him. The most I can do is to show my idea of the value of Cricket--the idea of one who has not excelled at it, but who has decided to practise it for all that it's worth. What *is* it worth? On the answer will depend the answer to the question, "Is it worth much training?" For myself, I unhesitatingly say "Yes." During the next two years I shall practise exercises for Cricket--for batting, bowling, and fielding; perhaps I shall not appear in any game or match at all till then. This must not be misunderstood. I shall focus my powers upon the exercises and practice, but before and afterwards I shall try to keep them and the game in proper perspective with reference to brain-work, character, the whole life. Others must do the same, and cultivate Cricket according as it shall seem likely to help with reference to these ends--not as first thing, I know; not as last thing, I hope, but wherever it shall aid the body-building and mind-building of a citizen of the British Empire and of the world. And let me add a word. I am not sure that you will ever find a more all-round exercise for the whole self, the whole *man* (including the "social animal" of Aristotle), than Cricket will be: it is not yet so, but will be if it is properly played and practised and trained for, *if*----

But if it is not properly done, if you don't watch the game properly, trying to get hints for use; if you don't ask for advice from the best professionals, experts, veterans, and spectators--they are the people; if you loaf in the field and will not be prompt to start and stretch and sprint and pick up and throw in, and safe "to have and to hold"; if you will not learn to bat with the help of your feet and legs (I don't mean your pads), as well as with a straight bat and forward left elbow; if you will not do exercises without which you cannot tell whether you will be a bowler or not; if you will not train, or give up anything, or study health at all; or, on the other hand, if you will not work, and do not feel inclined to; well, then, I shall say, Cricket is not worth much to you unless you are a born cricketer and also a born all-round boy or man. At the most it is an open-air occupation with a certain value for health, hardihood, discipline, social intercourse, but not much even of a recreation. At its best its physical results may and probably must develop corresponding intellectual and moral results, if not in this generation and in this life, then surely in the next.

CHAPTER VIII.

SPECIAL EXERCISES AND NOTES ON PRACTICE.

IF any reader can easily perform the various movements of Cricket as shown in the photographs and in the actual play of experts, he does not require special exercises for Cricket. But--if we may judge by results--he is the exception; he is the genius, the born player. How is it that we have so long tolerated Carlyle's ridiculous assertion, "Genius is an infinite capacity for taking pains"? This is just precisely what genius is not. In Cricket the genius-player plays correctly without taking pains, almost without taking thought. For such players this book is not written. It is written for beginners and others, to suggest certain exercises and practice and principles of practice which are not necessarily quite correct, but which are the best which some of the most successful models have hitherto enabled me to devise in order that care and art "may triumph over nature till art becomes natural." It is this second nature, this sedulously acquired nature, which now has become so much a part of myself at Tennis or Racquets that the sedulous attention is utterly denied by many. What I have done at these games, others can do at Cricket.

Is such practice worth while? will be the question asked here, as in the chapter on Training. Here, as there, the answer depends on whether Cricket well (or better) played is worth while? What is meant by Cricket well played? Enjoyment, health, physical and mental and moral education. If these are brought or increased by improvement, and if improvement results from such practice, then such practice is worth while. Only personal experiment can decide on the merits or demerits of the system; certainly it is economical of time as well as of money, since five or ten minutes a day are quite enough.

The part-by-part system of practice has been defended at some length in "The Training of the Body." American athletes use it with great energy and great success; examples are given in the chapter on Fielding. Mr. Edward Lyttelton, in his book on Cricket, remarks of the learner that "his principal task may be described as learning certain motions till they become habits...." While he frequently advises bedroom-practice with a bat and without a ball, he does not suggest bedroom-practice without a bat. Yet it is by such practice first of one part of the mechanism, then of another, that all the parts can be made good and easy and then by degrees be combined harmoniously together in good and easy strokes. Otherwise some part or parts will almost certainly be done wrongly.

For many of the strokes and other movements of Cricket are not natural--are even against the natural movements. The reader should study what Ranjitsinhji says on pp. 152 and 158 of his book (First Edition). He says: "Both batting and bowling call into play particular muscles" (I suppose he means "combinations of muscles") "which they alone can exercise." One might add wicket-keeping and fielding, with their quick stooping and stretching to this side or to that. Let the forward-stroke be again outlined, to show how little likely one is ever to master its mechanism without mastering the parts of it.

In order to smother a ball successfully by forward-play, one needs an eye to watch and observe intelligently and to send a report quickly and accurately to the brain, and then to watch again; this, and what will follow, one needs to have as nearly automatic as possible. One must have a good brain to order and ensure correct and well-timed and co-ordinated movements of the muscles; these include (1) a rapid and direct lunge of the left foot, slightly to the left of the approaching ball, and with the body-weight; (2) a firm right foot and straight right leg; (3) the head coming (with the body-weight) over the left foot; (4) a rapid and direct extension of left wrist, left elbow, left shoulder, the knuckles of the left hand leading the way, the fullest force to come at the instant when the bat shall strike the ball; (5) a straight bat (covering the wickets as much as possible); (6) preservation or rapid recovery of balance; (7) alertness to run forward, if necessary. These being some of the requisites, how many are likely to possess them merely through net-practice or games?

Of course some net-practice and games must come before and while the part-by-part system is tried, if only to give interest to the system, to show the difficulties of the game, to show the progress made, and--because human nature is as it is. But too many games by themselves will tend chiefly to accentuate and habituate the natural movements, which are faults. The probability of many faults--I myself had nearly all when I played--will be clear if we consider how many different classes of movements are involved in the stock-in-trade of a good all-round cricketer. We are so deluged by the general word "exercise," that we forget how many provinces it has, instead of being simply a matter of large biceps and power to lift weights. Such symptoms have little to do with success in Cricket; they may even have something to do with failure in so far as--for example--they bring with them slowness and neglect of the internal organs of the body. I notice that one book of "Physical Culture" suggests a series of strain-exercises as useful for batting, bowling, etc. I should consider these to be hindrances rather than helps. Imagine a person who should practise fast throwing, by movements against a strong resistance!

If only in order to expose the fallacy that every form of "exercise"--any and every exercise in a gymnasium or elsewhere--must be useful for the motions of Cricket, let us note

THE DIFFERENT CLASSES OF EXERCISES

which are demanded by Cricket as a "trinity of games," including the two very complex arts of batting (forward-play, driving, back-play, cutting, etc.), and of fielding (starting, running, catching, picking up, throwing in, etc.).

Fast full movements are to be found in all these departments of the game, as the photographs will show: for example, one often stretches out quickly to the full reach in forward-play, in overhand bowling, in fielding a ball nearly out of reach.

These and other features of play require not only a fast and full movement, but also an independent control of the various muscles in various combinations, and a rapid start.

Fast and partial (or arrested) movements are scarcely less important. Thus the batsman must be able to draw certain strokes up with a sharp jerk, lest he send a catch; the bowler to alter his action by using some part of his mechanism only slightly; the fielder to let go the ball at the right point during the action of the throw. The feint at boxing and at all games often requires this partial or arrested movement of some muscles, and therefore, again, independent control of these as well as a rapid start.

Some movements will be fast, some less fast, some quite slow. One should control the pace.

This must all be with balance: he who has played forward must immediately be ready to run; he who has bowled, to catch or field or get behind the wicket; he who has run to field a ball, to throw it in. "The ready," that is to say the most effective *point de depart,* must be lost either never or for the smallest possible fragment of time.

In the first class of movements we had extensions, say of the left arm in fielding, made fast and fully. Sometimes such extensions must be not only *made,* but also *held,* as when one stoops to field a ball with the left hand or stretches that hand out to make a high catch. At the end of this complete and sustained stretch there must be mastery of the mechanism: the hand must first yield slightly, then grasp safely.

Some strength is needed for forearm, wrist, thumb and fingers, etc. It is probable that strength is a quality to be acquired last, or at any rate after the rapid and ready and independent control of the muscles; lest prematurely elaborated strength and strain bring sluggishness and tardiness.

The numerous co-ordinations of muscles and muscle-groups (as outlined above, in the case of the forward stroke), must be under the sway of the well-timing eye which sends reports through the nervous system. Exercises are needed in observation as well as--to use technical language--in "quick and correct response to external stimulus," in "immediate and happy selection of harmoniously performing muscular combinations." To the accuracy of observation, and of choice of muscles, the senses of hearing and touch also contribute their share. Some expert players exercise them abundantly.

The imagination (based on the memory) must play an important part; aside from any picture-painting in the mind, of oneself as batting correctly but attackingly, bowling steadily but headily, fielding surely but briskly, one must have as a kind of background during the game the position of the wickets, the fielders, and so on.

It would be possible to classify the exercises differently. Thus we might consider, for example, running (ordinary starting and running forwards and backwards, sideways starting and sideways running forwards and backwards--no easy task--), jumping, bending, turning, lunging, stretching, and so on. There will be movements not only for the feet and legs and trunk, but also for the neck in various directions, for the shoulder (jerking and twisting), the whole arm, the forearm, the wrist, the fingers; if one studies three or four catches, one sees how many parts of the body are to be used.

But the feet and legs are the foundation. We hear much talk of the straight bat and the straight line of the bat's movement; but the feet and legs, their positions, their poise, their motions--these are the roots of success in Cricket as in Racquets and Tennis. I attribute nearly nine-tenths of my mistakes at these games to-day to mistakes made by the feet.

Last, but not least, we must mention the need for supplementary exercises. Cricket should be not only trained for, prepared for, and played, but also supplemented. Left-side exercises, in particular, should correct the balance upset by the excessive use of the right side.

Before we come to details, to actual exercises, we must first know how to do these exercises. A few hints on practice and its methods are indispensable. I crave the reader's patience while he listens to what may seem unpractical, but is really no less essential than the exercises themselves.

GENERAL HINTS ON THE EXERCISES AND ON PRACTICE.

The exercises which follow in the next section are not complete; they are samples which each reader should supplement as well as correct. There is need of individual observation here as everywhere; let every one be prepared to amend and to add. This will make my suggestions far more interesting and useful. For instance, let him watch how it is that men get out or send chances; let him watch (in games or from behind nets) each part of the stroke separately at first--the feet in particular. Let him ask professionals and other experts about the right pose and the right motion of each part.

Then let him practise part by part.

For if the whole movement consists of ten to twenty parts combined together, and if of these ten to twenty parts at least five to ten parts are naturally wrong, how can he ever learn the whole satisfactorily, how can he ever unlearn the wrong and learn the right whole, unless he unlearn the wrong and learn the right *parts*, one by one? As Mr. Edward Lyttelton says, "On the principle of doing one thing at a time, it is admissible in practice, especially at first, to concentrate the attention upon each requirement separately. He ought to do the one, but not leave the others undone!" Let me illustrate this. At one time I could not write an essay; *all* my essays were marked as very bad. Then I found out by degrees that essay-writing (like batting or fielding) was *a complex art*, and included, for me, the collection of true and useful ideas, the selection of those which were wanted, the underlining of the most important, the illustration of these by comparisons, contrasts, etc., the arrangement of these and the others, care for the beginning that it might be interesting, care for the ending that it might be impressive, and then--and not till then--the expression of the ideas, which was to be grammatical, clear, brief, forcible, appropriate, musical, and indeed full of virtues. All these processes can be considered separately; I believe that they can all be mastered separately; I believe that an essay can possess any one or two or more of these virtues without possessing the rest. I am trying to improve gradually in each process separately. This also has been my method for learning Racquets and Tennis and other games. I have called it the part-by-part method. A perfect whole is not a mere collection of perfect parts; it is a perfectly harmonious co-operation of perfect parts. The perfect parts must be combined. Yet the common sense of the reader will tell him that no perfect whole can possibly exist *unless every part* of it be perfect in itself. Let the genius do his work without knowing how; duffers like myself must be content to begin by separate control of the individual mechanisms. The combinations can be made later on.

Even if we insist on doing the whole as a whole, yet it is on each part in turn that we must concentrate our mind and focus our attention. Independent control must, as a general rule, precede the various combinations. Such concentration on each part in turn need not produce jerkiness: it has not done so (except at the beginning of the practice) where I have applied it. It has seemed rather to send more blood to the part used, to shorten the process of learning.

It is important that one should *at first look at the part which is being used,* till it can attend to itself by itself; that is, until it works easily and half-automatically. Or, if one likes, one can look at the reflection of that part in a mirror: this plan has its advantages. Choose whichever plan you prefer.

For every reason, including attention, slow and full breathing through the nose is essential to good practice.

Correctness must precede pace, and correctness with me has always demanded not only attention but also slowness at the start.

Pace is the next requisite. It comes to some extent with sheer repetition; but it must also be increased purposely. It must precede endurance and strength. For my own games I begin with no implement at all, so as to preserve freedom; then I use a handle; then the racket. I put speed and freedom and ease next after correctness.

Endurance can almost be left to take care of itself. The oftener one does an exercise correctly and attentively, the less easily tired the muscles will be.

Only one must not practise to excess. Before great fatigue or even before great boredom, the exercise should be stopped or changed. During the interval the newly-learnt movements will be more completely "assimilated." When the joints are well freed, the movements should be not only fast but also full--that is, complete in both directions, so as to empty out the capillaries of the muscles and allow fresh blood to flow in.

For the sake of economy of energy the unused parts should be loose and relaxed, not tight and tense.

Exercises done thus, with a brisk snap, and a staccatoed 1 --2 , or--for a forward-stroke--out--back, are far more valuable than the dull strength-and-strain grinding of many so-called physical culture schools.

These extensions of the muscles should be not simply made and then lost; they should be held for a second or two. This holding of the extreme limit of reach will be a wonderful help for batting, bowling, and fielding. Notice the full extensions in photographs.

The balance is to be recovered promptly or else not lost appreciably.

The different simple movements, thoroughly mastered, should be combined in twos, and then in threes, the complexity being increased gradually, but without the decrease either of correctness or of promptitude.

Strength--the power to lift or push or sustain heavy weights--is to come last of all. The wrist needs considerable strength, but it must not get that strength till after it has speed. Any strain that cramps one and makes one slow is undesirable for the mind as well as for the body.

Faults should be detected by another, or by means of comparison between photographs of experts and one's self in a looking-glass. Having detected the fault, correct it by concentrating the mind on the part concerned, and then *exaggerating the opposite fault*. Thus, if you are inclined to send catches in the slips, you are probably playing away to the left rather than straight at the ball. Find out which part of your mechanism is wrong; perhaps the left foot may be moving too much to the left. If so, then correct that by moving it purposely too much to the right. Find the error, and find the reason why it is an error.

Many short, sharp spells, with concentration, may be better than one long spell.

The maximum of air and light should be admitted into the exercising-place, and the minimum of clothing should be worn. There should be a good wash and rub afterwards.

There are many odd moments when wrist- or finger-exercises may be tried; or when a cricket-ball may be handled and fingered till it becomes a familiar friend. Thus the grips of Hirst (see the photographs) and others can be partially mastered in this way.

As to the imitation of others, authorities differ. Certainly I should say, Do not imitate any marked peculiarities until you have control of the chief muscles which you may have to use. It is only after mastering the complete mechanism that you are in a position to choose. Premature imitation is not advisable. Later on, it may be well to study some expert of about one's own build, and try whether certain of his habits are useful to oneself or not.

So far from urging that less attention be paid to the learning of Cricket, I urge that far more attention be paid to it *at the beginning,* if Cricket is to be played at all. I should like to see a few lessons thoroughly learnt; I should like to see these made interesting by biograph-mutoscope illustrations, especially of bowlers. A series of such illustrations would pay a Company well. The boys should watch these and then reproduce them. I should urge more attention *at the beginning; but, on the whole, less time.* A quarter of an hour's practice might often take the place of play or net-practice at the beginning. There would be increased economy of time, and afterwards increased skill and enjoyment. One would be training "Young England" in method.

We may now give samples of

ACTUAL EXERCISES,

referring the reader further to the special Chapters on Fielding, etc.

We have already insisted on the importance of foot-and-leg exercises in starting, running (sideways and backwards and forwards as well as straight forwards), jumping, bending, and stretching. The exercises lie at the roots of successful play, even if a few genius-players can bat well without them. For batting one needs in particular the sideways-running with the straight right leg as the basis of action.

The body-swing upon the hips, with powerful play of the muscles round the shoulder, is scarcely less useful in all three departments of the game: it has been described in a previous chapter. Every fast bowler knows how his back under his arms (especially the latissimus dorsi muscles) aches after his first day of practice.

The shoulders should be jerked up, down, backwards, forwards; and also rotated. To keep both shoulders always back is not the ideal for a cricketer, who must be able to move either shoulder in any direction which the joints and muscles allow. If one feels the shoulders of good players while they go through the action of batting (including the cut of some players), bowling, and fielding, one is amazed at the amount of work that they do, work for which the arm and wrist get much of the credit.

The forearm also requires to be jerked powerfully and fully, especially by the action (as already described) of whipping a peg-top.

Full extensions of the arm are to be made in various directions: for example, one should reach up, down, out, across. They should be made, and then *held*. At the end of them should be added some action of the fingers. It must be remembered that the wrist and fingers have to do not a little work at the full extension, whether in bowling or in fielding or (occasionally) in batting. Let the wrist-joint go the full distance; beyond that point let it move about, and let the fingers move about.

The hand needs to be shaken out as if it were a flag at the end of a stick. Then let it be exercised in various directions. First let there be the freedom, next the fast and full movements in each direction, next the partial movements.

Finger-exercises can be tried at any vacant moment. The other hand can help to free them and stretch them and strengthen them by resistance: for here, as with the wrist, one does need some strength, some straining power, against the ball or bat.

Massage is useful throughout these exercises, but is most easily applied to the fingers. "Deposits," which are causes and signs of fatal stiffness, may thus be removed, while the use of oil rubbed in, and attention to diet, will hasten the cure. The heat-treatment (known as the "baking-cure"), and the electric-light treatment, are both to be recommended.

Each finger should be exercised and developed separately, but the first finger in particular, for the sake of batting as well as bowling: the bat sometimes is held chiefly if not solely by this finger and the thumb. The full extensions and full flexions should be eventually both fast and strong, and also independent of the wrist-movements, so that for instance, while the bowler's wrist is still or putting on one break, his fingers may move or be putting on another break, with intent to deceive. The thumb must not be neglected. It can be freed and extended and strengthened by the aid of the other hand.

As we suggested just now, a ball should occasionally be held in the otherwise idle fingers, a Lawn Tennis ball being at first preferable until the fingers have stretched and grown powerful. Various grips and movements should thus become familiar. A box-full of old balls might be used in order to practise bowling or fielding: the Lawn Tennis ball exhibits the effects of a break or curl in the air far more clearly than a Cricket ball. The practice may be by the player himself against a wall, or with another player, a stump being put between the two, and a third player acting as wicket-keep.

There should be practice of alertness, of control of the body's weight, after each set of large muscle movements. For Racquets and Tennis I often practise in my bedroom a hard service of one kind or another, and then I immediately recover that waiting position from which I must be prepared to start in almost any direction *at once.* I suppose that skating must be almost the ideal training for weight-control.

The following exercises may be found very useful for various reasons: Peg-top whipping, some ball-game exerciser (like the patent for Lawn Tennis, but adapted to Cricket), Fencing, Boxing, Bartitsu, Hockey, Golf, Racquets, Tennis, Lawn Tennis, Fives, Squash, hopping and skipping.

These are merely suggestions. Each reader is urged to devise his own means of exercise. Let him work on the lines that Mr. C. B. Fry so admirably lays down in an article in the "Strand." He says, with reference to his high jumping: "I believe what did me more good than anything else was doing standing jumps regularly, every morning, over a big arm-chair in my room;" and, again: "Although, like most other footballers, I improved in value in some respects after I left school, and became heavier and stronger, I have never since been able to kick as neatly and accurately as I could then. I put this down partly to the constant practice we used to have at school in kicking a football about at odd hours, on a piece of ground called the paddock, and partly to the constant playing of what we called 'yard football.' We used to play this game in the asphalt yards attached to our houses, wearing tennis shoes and using an indiarubber ball about a third the size of a football. This game made one very accurate and quick with one's feet. I have often wished since I could get the same sort of practice."

Mr. Edward Lyttelton is equally to the point, when he remarks: "The truth must be insisted on; many a cricket match has been won in the bedroom. And even with the ball a good deal may be done. I could name two eminent batsmen who used, as boys, to wait till after the day's play was over, and the careless crowd had departed, and in the pavilion gave ten minutes or a quarter of an hour to practising a particular style of defence, about which more anon; the one bowled fast sneaks along the floor to the other, at about ten paces distance. This, too, yielded fruit in its time. Like all other great achievements, the getting a score against good bowling is the result of drudgery, patiently, faithfully borne. But the drudgery of cricket is itself a pleasure, and let no young cricketer suppose that he can dispense with it, though some few gifted performers have done great things with apparently little effort."

Besides the exercises outlined here, each player should certainly use *supplementary* exercises, especially for the breathing muscles, the abdominal muscles, the erector spinae, and the trapezius. So many of them are needed to correct deformities that I prefer not to offer any samples here. Some system should be chosen which gives exercises graduated according to the individual.[6]

The left side needs to be used in exercises and in games. A few words must be said about this much-neglected half.

The left side probably should not be trained up to the same pitch of excellence and versatility as the right side. Not only are some of the organs on the two sides different (for example, the stomach, liver, and heart), but apparently the supply of blood to the two sides is not equal. On the other hand, our present neglect and consequent atrophy of the left side is scandalously unfair and obviously disastrous in its general results on health and physique. Even for Cricket alone, we require the left side for fielding, and (far more than most people imagine) for batting, especially in forward-play. Moreover, there should be more than one left-hand bowler in each team. Such a bowler's ball approaches the batsman from an unusual direction and with an unusual break, tending to elicit catches on the off-side. The Americans, led by Professor Tadd, have shown that the left arm can draw and model and do other things practically as well as the right; and the majority of children brought up on Tadd's principles are nearly ambidextrous.

But how can *we* become left-handed? Well, apart from left-side exercises, and such forms of sport as Boxing and Fives, we can employ the left hand in opening doors, cutting bread, and so on. Occasionally left-handed games and matches would certainly vary the dulness of a season's Cricket--and this will apply equally to Lawn Tennis and other games.

But at present we are too truly a stiff-legged people, slow to start; as well as a one-sided people, not masters of our full forces. The reason for mental stupidity and atrophy must be partly physical. Brain-work alone--especially such as we are generally offered as intellectual "education"--is little likely by itself to remove such national faults.

A word may be said in conclusion, with reference not to "educators" but to teachers of Cricket.

While teaching a beginner, let them insist on the essential elements of good play, and give the reason why those elements are essential. Why not flourish the bat? Why not draw the right foot away to the leg-side? The answers to such questions are most helpful, and are very likely to induce a player to correct mistakes when otherwise he might not be convinced that he was radically wrong or know how he was radically wrong.

The practice of part-by-part should be encouraged, Mr. Edward Lyttelton's hints about bedroom exercise being constantly borne in mind. The movements should be explained and illustrated and *performed* by the teacher not only as complex wholes but also as simple parts. The teacher should say, for example, "Watch my left foot while I play forward. No; stand behind me, and watch its line. Now watch my left elbow." He should at first work slowly. Comparisons and contrasts are among the best of helps. Compare cutting to peg-top whipping; compare the left-foot lunge to the fencing lunge; contrast the alertness of the fielder and (if he have Abel's activity) of the batsman with the fixed "stance" of the golfer, whose eye must not follow the ball's flight at once.

Let the teacher urge the beginner to correct his faults by exaggerating in the opposite direction: if the batsman's right leg inclines to bend itself, let it be kept rigidly stiff, ridiculously straight.

Individuality must not be crushed. But it must not be fostered unless the player already has the necessary mechanisms of the various parts of play--batting and bowling--under control. The player must not hope to form his style out of a stock-in-trade consisting of less than half the muscular elements which practically *every* successful player possesses. The genius-player may safely be left to move along his own lines, with occasional supervision. The duffer-player, like myself, must not be left to do so; first he must learn to use those muscles, and especially those large muscles, which the best players use--for example, in forward-play, the full extension of right leg and left wrist. Then, if I may repeat the old metaphor, having mastered the spelling and the vocabulary, let him at length write his own writing; having collected the bricks and mortar and wood, let him at length build his own building.

CHAPTER IX.

FALLACIES OF THEORISTS AND OTHERS.

IT is safe to presume that every reader has read some one or more of the many writings on Cricket (from a penny upwards); that he has seen many good matches and many great amateur as well as professional experts; that he has batted often, fielded often, bowled at least once. So there need be no explanation of the game and its divisions; the reader already knows pretty shrewdly the chief merits of batting, fielding, and bowling, at least when he sees these merits. He rather needs to have fallacies exposed and faults explained. This chapter will clear the ground of rubbish after we have begun to sow advice upon it; the ground must be cleared, even if it be necessary to pull down some old ruins surviving from fifty years ago.

The first fallacy is about games in general, and about Cricket in particular as the grandest of them all. And here we must distinguish what our games *are* to some few, from what they *can* and *should be* to many if not to all. We shall claim much for them as the British nation claims much for itself--on the strength of its best examples, without imagining that the full advantages are universally, or even generally, realised. For the fallacy of many good players, that Cricket actually is all that can be claimed for ideal Cricket, rather than that it might and should be all this, is no less ridiculous. If, for example, the fielder stands careless and listless, Cricket becomes for him almost an exercise in non-promptitude! The ball runs to the side of him, his lazy flop towards it is almost an exercise in non-extension as well. We must guard against all extreme statements as to what cricket is. It certainly is not an end in itself. Even all-round success in it is not an end in itself; still less is success in some one branch only. But it is as well for all who play Cricket to remind themselves if not of the ideal yet of what is higher than their present actual.

Cricket is not merely a muscle-maker, a sort of gymnastic drill which scarcely trains the nerves at all. To run out to a ball, to stand up to a fast bowler and not draw away the right foot, to field a hard drive, this means nerve. Nor is Cricket merely a physical health-maker or disease-palliator. To have practised and played it properly is quite impossible without some mental and moral exercise and health as well; it is a social game of the best kind--it is a great bond of union. Far above brainless frivolity, farther above mere recreation, it can be a preparation for the whole of life, even for business life; for it can teach co-operation, specialisation, patience, observation, promptness, full extension, use of great weight and power without loss of poise. It can be valuable for all life, which mere muscle-straining without nerve-training, mere disease-avoidance, mere amusement, cannot possibly be.

There are those who would not deny to Cricket some of these many merits, but they would say that Cricket can only be played properly by born players, that no others can ever play it well. To fielding this certainly does not apply: fielders can be trained; so can batsmen, up to a certain point; so--for all we know--can bowlers. I do not mean by the present absence of method, but by the use of sensible methods.

For the common advice of the genius-players who are so often set to teach the game is little likely to make cricketers. "Play in a natural way," they say. This advice must be exposed, though it is insisted upon by some of the leading authorities. For Cricket is not a natural game. As Ranjitsinhji aptly says, the natural tendency is to hit up and to pull to the on. In playing forward one does not naturally keep the bat straight and with its handle nearer to the bowler than its bottom is; one does not naturally keep the right foot still, send the left elbow forward, and the bat near to the left foot. The instinct is against all this--for example, to keep the striking implement well away from one's body, as at Golf, Lawn Tennis, Tennis, Racquets, Squash, Fives, Hockey, and so on. Conversely, Mr. Lacey, the Secretary of the M.C.C., after having the Cricket-habit ingrained in him, found it hard at Tennis to get far enough away from the ball. And how can bowling be considered "natural" for him whose fingers and back-muscles are practically undeveloped? So our answer to the teacher who would say, "Choose the natural way of batting, or of bowling, or of fielding," is that this may be well enough if you already have control of the different parts of your batting, or bowling, or fielding mechanism; but that otherwise (and the chances otherwise are at least ten to one), the undeveloped muscles will probably be unused; the work will be thrown on other muscles, and will be done either badly or with excessive effort. We should prefer to say this: "Get control of the various muscles, as by the fast full-movement[7] system; then get the foundations of play--the right foot as pivot, the left leg as straight lunger (for forward strokes), the straight bat with left elbow well forward, the habit of the eye on the ball, and so on; then, if you like, by all means try different ways and styles, and choose what is natural to you; but--unless you are a prodigy--do not be natural prematurely, or you will almost surely form bad habits."

That practice of this kind or indeed any sort of training will not be worth while, is a fallacy that has been exposed at the beginning of the chapter on Training. Even if Cricket led to nothing at all, training would still be as useful as most things that we attend to. But Cricket can make one fitter for all-round activity, and proper practice and training must make one fitter for Cricket--fitter in skill, fitter in endurance, fitter in every way.

It is necessary to secure *proper* practice, not practice based on mere theory. Many theories are egregious fallacies. Let us consider a few of them on the art of batting.

The first is that in forward play the bottom of the bat must never be sent forward beyond the left foot.[8] In this, as in most theories, there are germs of truth, namely (a), that not many can stretch out much further than this without undue strain or loss of balance; (b) that very few can get pace and power at all into the stroke beyond their left foot, and that therefore the above is a safe rule for the attacking drive; (c) that the ball should usually be hit when the bat is not further forward than this. But the theory--which is repeated by most writers on the game--utterly ignores one or two undoubted facts, (i.) First of all it seems a general principle of ball-games that to ensure a straight line of stroke (and also to allow for too early a stroke), one must *follow-through* some way with the implement; this is especially true of the ordinary forward stroke, which is usually played by faith as well as by sight; (ii.) the defensive and "safety" forward-stroke (when it is distinct from the attacking drive) has as its first object to smother the ball, to get near to the pitch of it, before the break works out its fulness; common sense would urge a player, if he could do so, to add an extra foot or so to his reach; (iii.) both Shrewsbury and Abel (see the photographs, which show them after the ball would have been hit) do actually reach far beyond the left foot. Who is to limit an Abel, if he has the litheness to add to his stretch those cubits which he cannot add to his stature? The decision seems to be one for the individual. If he can stretch out thus without tilting up the bottom of his bat (and so lifting the ball), and without straining himself or tumbling over, then by all means let him do so, for he will crush the ball thus. But if he cannot, then let him do what he has been so often told to do.

Similarly in Tennis I have been frequently told to keep the head of my racket above the level of my wrist for ordinary strokes. Latham does not; Fennell does not; Fairs does not; Lambert did not; Pettitt of course does not; Charles Saunders, Alfred Tompkins, and Mr. Alfred Lyttelton do. I will not deny the beauty and grace and power of the so called "correct" stroke; but what I maintain is that most of us cannot afford the risk. We want to meet the ball as long as possible in its own line. We prefer safety and efficiency to risk and theory: as to grace, well, Latham and Fennell are quite good enough for me.

It is often said that the secret of successful batting is the straight bat. There is a fallacy here; the straight bat is important for many strokes, but the straight moving line of the bat, the direct line in which it meets the approaching ball, this is important also; and scarcely less important, for forward play, is the straight lunge of the left foot near the bottom of the bat. I would set this as a foundation of good forward play, since with the left foot goes much of the body's weight, and since otherwise there is a gap between bat and leg.

A third and very grievous fallacy about batting is that the right foot must be kept still. Some have urged that it should be pegged down. Here also is a germ of truth. The right foot is the aphorme, the pivot, for most strokes, the late cut excepted. And the line of the right foot, a line just outside the leg-stump, is usually to be kept to; that foot must not be drawn away cowardly towards short leg. But as a universal law "the unmoved right foot" is a mistake. Even in forward play it often tends to drag slightly (it must not drag over the crease), and the heel may rise from the ground. More obvious exceptions are when a batsman runs out (as Abel is doing in one illustration), or jumps out (as Shrewsbury is doing in another). Why should we fetter active-footed boys or men by restrictions that apply well enough to staid men with a long reach. "Play with the feet," says Abel to all who have feet to play with. If I can take the sting off a Racquet service by four or five steps forward, which will make it a volley or half-volley, why not? This is not rash: it is frequently defensive. I dare not wait! For the late cut, again, I believe every player moves his right foot across. For the glide I believe every player moves his right foot back, not a few move their right foot across also. For the pull of a short ball, the right leg, as in the illustration of Hirst, may go well across. For playing back I observe that nearly every good player, including W. G. Grace (see the photograph of him in Ranjitsinhji's book), does move his right foot more or less towards his own wicket; this gives an extra fraction of time in which to watch the short ball and its break or rise. Moreover, the retiring of the right foot does actually prepare for the back play.

A fourth batting fallacy is that the late cut is with the wrist *only*. One writer after another repeats this in the face of the practice of nine late-cutters out of every ten whom I have ever seen. Here once more is a germ of truth, that the wrist is often a *sine qua non*. But few could get much power with the wrist alone. As a proof, keep your whole body stiff except your wrist, and then try to cut. Is that how most experts play? Or imitate their exact stroke for half an hour, and see if you do not ache in your forearm and perhaps your shoulder too. Or strip, and watch your muscles in a mirror. We do really want nude photographs for these strokes. Even Shrewsbury uses much besides his wrist. Some wrist there is, though there need not be here any more than when one shakes out a clotted stylographic pen. In the average late cut the body moves a bit to put in some weight; the back muscles under the arm-pits (latissimus dorsi) do some work; the shoulder jerks a little or a lot; the forearm jerks powerfully; some players add force by the stepping of the right foot and the straightening of the left leg; some--these are probably few--keep an almost or quite rigid wrist. Plenty of strength and pace will come from the other muscle-groups. In fact, for the ordinary beginner I should urge a reliance upon the large muscles in particular, lest the big bat shall nearly wield the boy as the big tail nearly waggled the dog.

A similar fallacy exists in Racquets. It is supposed that Pettitt relies almost entirely on his wrist-flick; and this certainly has an astounding force. But with it there almost invariably go a forearm-jerk and a shoulder-jerk. Latham's Racquet-stroke largely depends on these two factors as well as on the wrist-flick.

That the pull is a bad stroke is a dying fallacy. It is not a bad stroke so long as it is a safe stroke. At times it appears to me to be the safest stroke, if only because it meets the ball nearly in its own line and, as Shrewsbury says, need not send the ball near any fielder; the bottom of the bat may rise, and thus an extra foot or so may be given to the reach. The pull is chiefly bad if tried with the wrong ball, especially a fast and straight ball, or if tried in the wrong way--for example, without the lunge forward of the left foot as in the photograph of Abel (that one may get near the pitch of the ball), or the backward step of the right foot, as in the photographs of Hirst and Shrewsbury (that one may see more of the way of the ball); or if tried by the wrong man--a man with no eye.

Another dying fallacy is that to run out is a mark of rashness. I have already compared the steps forward in order to take a heavily-cut

Racquet service; in Tennis also we have a similar safety or killing stroke; and in Lawn Tennis the player who comes up to the net to volley is not necessarily rash. The safest stroke in the whole game is the ordinary full-pitch; next to it comes the ordinary long-hop; next to it the ball that allows one to get well to the pitch of it. The safety-player can often secure either the first or the third by an apparently mad jump out of his ground. As a foreigner once said, "When you've got a good boxer against you, it's wisest to hit him before he's ready."

Leaving the time-honoured but misguided advice about batting, let us turn to the mistakes about bowling. Here we have the fatal opinion that, unless the bowler who has found an easy swing bowls well, he is not likely ever to become a good bowler at all. I should rather forbid any player to despair until he has mastered first the mechanism of bowling by fast full movements and extensions; till then perhaps he has failed because he has not fairly used the back-muscles under the arm-pits (how they ache after a day of bowling), the shoulder-jerk, the wrist-movements, the finger-movements--especially those of the first finger. It is great folly not to be controller of these parts of the bowling-apparatus before one has decided either on one's individual action or on one's incapacity to bowl.

Similarly, in fielding, Cricket suffers from many ignorances and negligences. Not only is there the general idea that fielding is unimportant compared with batting and bowling, but it is assumed that it can be got through somehow without practice or apprenticeship. The mere art of patient yet expectant waiting for an opportunity is in itself almost as difficult to acquire as it is worth acquiring. Mere safety in stopping balls, or even in catching balls, is often considered the acme of excellence, whereas the anticipation is not less essential. Here also, as in bowling, a boy or man is wont to adopt a (?) style without having first learnt and, as it were, infibred within him the A B C of success and enjoyment; to start hither or thither in a moment, to make a full stretch hither or thither, to keep the balance, to throw in at once and accurately--not one player in a hundred has gone through his apprenticeship.

Or, if a boy or man does field reasonably well in one place, he is contented. He does not aim at being able to field passably in other places. As to wicket-keeping, that he never dreams of. And yet how else is he likely to learn to field at short slip, or to take balls he has bowled?

Then there is the watching--how dull it appears to the members of the batting side who are out or not yet in! Many would rather be fielding--and what more need be said? Yet here is another misconception. Watch the play, as Shrewsbury does, or watch it part by part, with a view of getting hints as to what to avoid and what to practise, and you henceforth find the inalienable interest.

This failure to watch the play part by part--say the batsman's feet first, then his bat, and so on--finds its parallel in practice, which is seldom part by part. People play in matches, in practice-games, at the nets; but it is always with full implements. Is it not great stupidity to imagine that the game itself is the best practice for strokes? The very variety militates against the mastery of *any one* thing *par excellence*. Were it not better sometimes to play stump-cricket or "snob-cricket"--an india-rubber ball can be used; to practise jumping with preservation of balance (see Shrewsbury); sideway running (see Abel); straight-forward lunges with balance and rapid recovery, with right foot scarcely moving, with right leg unbent; or left foot lunges alone, then the bat lunges as well; to throw a Lawn Tennis ball up against a wall and on its recoil play it with a straight bat and prominent left elbow; to go through the action of cutting, and cut-driving; to do wrist-movements; to imitate the whipping of a peg-top; to start quickly in every direction in turn; to shift the weight; to extend the arms up, down, to the sides; to pick up and throw a real ball (or an imaginary ball, in a bedroom); to hold one's hands for a catch here or there, whether of an imaginary ball or of one thrown or hit off a wall; to develop the left side; and so on? Is it not the most grievous and fatal fallacy to rely on and to urge others to rely on nothing but practice at the nets or the game itself, even if these are indispensable?

I have already exposed the fallacy[9] that to practise part by part is necessarily to produce a jerky and disjointed stroke; at first it may do so, but eventually the parts will easily combine into a unity, if we do them rightly. My own Tennis and Racquet strokes are no longer jerky and disjointed, but once they were so. Use has fused the parts into a whole.

Quite apart from success and enjoyment in Cricket, the game demands these and many other exercises, not only as apprenticeship, and as corrective of faults, but also as supplementary. For the last fallacy which we expose is that Cricket as played at present is at all a complete exercise for the body. A few reforms will be suggested in a subsequent chapter.

CHAPTER X.

MERITS OF CRICKET.

CRICKET as she is played does not bear one tithe of her possible fruits; the soil is not properly prepared for her; she is left to grow anyhow. This is a sad error, if only because she is not a natural game--a game of natural movements. What more unnatural is there for most of us than to play forward correctly? The same applies to most games, for example to Lawn Tennis. Here we must consider the advantages of Cricket not as the practice and play now are, but as they easily *might be, if all-round Cricket were well prepared for and taught, well practised and played;* learnt and cultivated with science, not haphazardly; in moderation, not too little, not too much; with conscious care at the start, until conscious correct care has begotten sub-consciously correct ease.

The first advantage of the game, as it should be, is economy. If it only saves doctors' and druggists' bills, it is worth its cost in time and money. Professionals earn a healthy living by Cricket. Many schoolmasters, many clerks and partners, owe their position largely to their Cricket. This is but common sense. To play Cricket well is at least as good a qualification as to know well the names and dates of many prophets, kings, battles, and other dull trivialities.

For Cricket should develop the intellect. Quite apart from the effect of bodily health and activity upon brain-work, quite apart from the tonic of recreation and change of employment, Cricket should give lessons for life: it should teach co-operation, division of labour, encouragement of individuality; it should teach the art of mastering the mechanisms, the A B C, so indispensable to success; it should foster observation, rapid decision, then rapid action, judgment by results, memory, foresight. It *should*--though it seldom *does*. This intellectual aspect of Cricket is of national importance. We need intelligent leaders and workers: Cricket might easily be made to produce them. We need such in war as in peace: as Ranjitsinhji insists, "after all, Cricket is warfare in miniature. It is man against man, general against general," and, we may add, team against team.

To pass from the intellectual to the physical advantages which are so closely connected with them, Mr. Edward Lyttelton says:

"It is impossible to make twenty runs in decent style without giving evidence of bodily pluck, readiness of resource, patience, health, strength and training." But here again we must distinguish what *is* from what might and should be. Cricket should encourage general health and training, general fitness (most excellent word), the power to preserve life, not only by its exercise and physical virtues, but also by the movements of muscles, by the air, light, scenery, subsequent washing, which can all improve the well-being, not completely yet conspicuously.

The enjoyment--if only we were better trained to enjoy the game--must affect the blood in the most favourable way, as the chemical experiments of Professor Gates, of Washington, have demonstrated, in the American "Medical Times" for December, 1897. We thank God better by genuine enjoyment than by mere word of mouth.

The word "aesthetic" is used in two senses--in reference to enjoyment, and in reference to artistic beauty and gracefulness. Cricket should be an "aesthetic" game in both senses. When properly prepared for and played and supplemented, it should produce a body pleasant to behold whether in motion or at rest--a "kinetic" and "dynamic" and "static" pleasantness to the eye. The senses also should have their interesting growth by Cricket; the sight by the timing and by the use of the imagination; the hearing; the touch; the muscular sense.

Of the moral and spiritual effects we need not say much. It seems to me to be here that Cricket *does* do much that it *should* do. Honour, sympathy and courtesy, pluck, patience, good temper, these are a few of the qualities that do often result.

Clearest of all, however, is the social value as a tie and connecting link between individuals and groups both small and great. Rudyard Kipling, with all his genius for seeing and describing things imperial, scarcely realised the function of Cricket as a common ground for meeting and forming friendships, quite aside from its advantages in opening the mind by journeys among near or distant people. What Ranjitsinhji so aptly remarks in reference to the classes within England herself can be applied also to the relation between any sets of people anywhere. He says:

"It is a grand thing for people who have to work most of their time to have an interest in something or other outside their particular groove. Cricket is a first-rate interest. The game has developed to such a pitch that it is worth taking interest in. Go to Lord's and analyse the crowd. There are all sorts and conditions of men there around the ropes--bricklayers, bank-clerks, soldiers, postmen, and stockbrokers. And in the pavilion are K.C.'s, artists, archdeacons, and leader-writers. Bad men, good men, workers and idlers are all there, and all at one in their keenness over the game. It is a commonplace that cricket brings the most opposite characters and the most diverse lives together. Anything that puts many very different kinds of people on a common ground must promote sympathy and kindly feelings. The workman does not come away from seeing Middlesex beating Lancashire or *vice versa* with evil in his heart against the Upper Ten; nor the Mayfair *homme de plaisir* with a feeling of contempt for the street-bred masses. Both alike are thinking how well Mold bowled, and how cleanly Stoddart despatched Briggs' high-tossed slow ball over the awning."

This is pre-eminently true. Cricket already is, and can be to an even greater extent, a healthy interest that is a grand bond of union for the nation, and yet not (like so many religious, commercial, educational, and other bonds) a frequent cause of separation from other nations.

What is Cricket to you? That is a very different question from "What might, can, should Cricket be to you?" We have answered part of the latter question. Before answering the former let us take some contrasts. What already exists that can be compared to Cricket in regard to effects? Gymnastics, strength-and-strain-exercises; card-games, other games (Lawn Tennis, Ping-Pong, Golf, etc.); "economical" education--where is any teaching about such lessons as co-operation to be found in England? It is to be found in America, but with it is also to be found the terrible money-grubbing and grabbing spirit; "intellectual" education--sum up the useful results of what one has learnt in school: nine-tenths of it I pray that I may forget; physical and hygienic education--where is it? Not at home, not at school, not in business, not in society; in Cricket there is quite a supply of such education, mainly of an unconscious kind; enjoyment, gracefulness, pure and wholesome cultivation of the senses--where are they? Education about pure and wholesome and kindly social and national relations--where is it? Even moral and spiritual education by preaching and teaching. Compare and contrast these and other means of education for physique, for character, for life, with Cricket as she is, and then with Cricket as she might and should be. Judge the advantages of Cricket for yourself as an individual and as a member of many groups.

The present advantages of Cricket would be increased ten-fold if more care were taken by those in authority. Cricket needs greater interest and attractiveness for the majority of players; it needs better basic preparation for all departments of play; it needs supplementation by other exercises and other means to health. By itself it is not, never will be, never can be, a complete education. Of course not. But properly cultivated, with other things, in its proper place, it seems to me splendid. If it seems so to the reader, then let him give it a care, let him cultivate it, *in proportion to its all-round value in his eyes.*

CHAPTER XI.

SUGGESTED REFORMS.

AS with other games like Tennis and Racquets, so with Cricket, we may assume that *the game as now played is excellent for experts who either have wealth and leisure or else are professionals*. For those, and for others at intervals, let the play be nearly as it now is. Let the best go on. Let there be test-matches, county and 'varsity matches, college and school matches, house and dormitory matches, and so on. Here we deal chiefly with reforms outside these decisive games which are likely to remain as they are.

With those who are not experts of the classes mentioned above, the play cries for adaptation. First of all, there is need for snob-cricket, stump-cricket, room-cricket (not mere bedroom practice, but an actual game), as a more regular and more enjoyable substitute. Secondly, there is need for preparation; Cricket has been described as a trinity of games, and the stump-practice suggested in a previous chapter can serve as a preparation for fielding. The exercises offered in other chapters would serve as substitutes and also as preparation for play when play itself was out of the question. Cricket is a river that needs a good source and many good tributary-streams; it needs preparatory exercises and games. Such practice would soon make the play itself far more pleasant and interesting. Thirdly, there is need of supplementation--for example, left-handed play, the use of the left side being important, not merely in fielding (what crocks most people are with their left hands!), but in change-bowling also. Why should not more players be able to bowl an over or two left-handed for a change?

Besides this, there is need of cheapness--of economy of money and of time as well, so that each player may get more work to do and less dull waiting.

Above all, there is need of some "fun for the duffers," if the game is to spread or even to hold its own. We are rapidly becoming Americanised. No longer do the majority care to serve merely as watchers, or at the best as ninepins to a Hirst or a Rhodes, as feeders and throwers-in for an Abel, a Shrewsbury, a Fry, or a Ranji. They want to be up and doing and enjoying themselves, or else they will give up the so-called play in disgust; it *isn't* play. That is their true complaint.

And so we say, let the best players and the other players at intervals have their matches and games and net-practice as before, with any changes that may be accepted (such as those which will be touched on directly). But let there be *something* to give pleasure to the average person, whether it be an occasional game of tip-and-run, or an occasional game with some sort of a handicap.

What the handicap shall be, whether more men in the field, or both sides fielding, or fewer men on the stronger side, or smaller bats, or larger wickets, or a time-limit, must be left to the players themselves to decide. Only, one could wish for a more democratic and representative vote instead of the whole management being left to the few experts or "aristocrats," who, of course, will legislate from their own point of view.

The reforms suggested by so many writers do not really deal with the masses of cricketers at all. The time-limit for the innings (it might be annulled in case of a difficult wicket), the running out of boundary hits, the declaring of the innings closed at any moment, the innings of sections of sides at a time--these things do not tend to make Dick, Tom, and Harry really enjoy themselves or improve their play appreciably more than at present.

As contrasted with short games of stump-cricket (to encourage accuracy of batting and to develop new bowlers), and with the building of clubs having plain rooms for evening games, such reforms are trifling except for the very few who play well. It would be far better to tell people how to field, or even how to watch with a view to interest and improvement. Reforms must aim at giving amusement, interest, attractiveness to the play of the average cricketer.

Let us consider a common experience in a one-day College match at Cambridge, putting aside the wet or rather the difficult wicket on which every player gets a knock; we want to think of Cricket at its best--on a fine day and a good wicket. The side that wins the toss sends in its first two or three bats; they pile up some hundreds of runs; the other members sit and do nothing; the captain eventually declares; the opposing side, after its hours of "country life," has no chance of winning, so the players either stick and try to play out time, or else make a desperate attempt and slog at everything like a set of Jessops, but unskilled. No wonder there is apathy.

We begin by pointing out what appears at first to be the most ridiculous change; yet it is certain that when the tail of a team *does* go in, then it wants to enjoy itself for more than a few brief seconds. If the captain will not every now and then absolutely reverse the order of going in (at least at the end of a day's scouting), then let the tail improve its own batting. The improvement rests with the members themselves. Let them begin practice on any level piece of ground, with a soft ball and a stick (to emphasise the importance of the straight bat); or let them in private (if not in a new form of drill) lunge with the left foot, stretch straight forward with the head and left-wrist and elbow, move the right foot across and cut with shoulder, forearm, and wrist, repeat the body-swing, and so on. The drill could be made less dull if one individual "set" the exercises to the rest, at first simple movements, then more complex movements with varied pace. Let the players give themselves the best possible chance of a reasonably long innings when they *do* go in. Let them make runs somehow,[10] not neglecting the safest kind of pull, for example, merely because it is called "bad style."

More important than attention to batting is attention to bowling. We need not allow a "free margin" to bowlers of doubtful action; there are other remedies. Why should not people learn to make the ball curl in the air, starting their experiments with a Lawn Tennis ball, which gives more marked effects. That which is done habitually by Baseball throwers, and occasionally if unintentionally by a few bowlers, can surely be done frequently and intentionally by many bowlers, if only there be careful and thorough research. But anyhow let the breaks be learnt; let the first finger and the wrist be trained to strong movements of various kinds. Let the young players be given small bats and balls to play with. Let them and older players be given an over now and then for a change in less important games. Certainly let the various mechanisms of bowling be mastered before a player decides that he has not the gift of bowling; let him do arm-and-shoulder extensions (see the photographs of Hirst), wrist-turns, and so on; and then (as suggested above), practise with a stump, a wicket-keeper, and another bowler on the other side of the stump; let each have his little paper-marks on the ground, and let him pitch the ball as near as he can to these. Let every would-be bowler, that is to say every cricketer, try to bowl round the wicket, if only in the old style with the low delivery (like W. G.'s, as described by Mr. A. G. Steel). Or let him try his luck with lobs, if only that he may learn how to make the ball break both ways. Let him see if he cannot bowl a little with his left-hand--who knows? We *must* raise the number of bowlers as well as the standard of bowling. On that point all are agreed.[11]

Perhaps at the same time the power of the batsman might be lessened,[12] either by a number-limit or a time-limit to the innings, or by a smaller bat (narrower and thicker), or by a larger wicket (higher or broader, or both--at the moment when I write this, the suggested change has not been accepted by all--), or, better still, by the following plan. On a caking wicket we do not need to shorten the batsman's innings, except to put a stop to excessive poking. The ground takes whatever break is put on (and perhaps adds some of its own). Why should there not be an artificial material which would take a good deal of break and not be dangerous. The M.C.C. out of its abundance might offer a reward (say of PS100) to the inventor of some material, which need not extend over more than a small area. We want a floor that will show just what twist or spin has been given to the ball, so that inferior batsmen shall not now make their centuries merely because the ball will not "bite." In Racquets, Tennis, covered-court Lawn Tennis, and Ping-Pong, the ball performs practically whatever antics it ought to perform. We want a pitch that will carry out the bowler's work without adding or subtracting *much*. Neither a plumb wicket nor a caking wicket does that. We need some such material as Mr. W. J. Ford suggests, perhaps a kind akin to cokernut matting.

The proposed leg-before-wicket reform by which the batsman is given out if, in the opinion of the umpire, the ball would have struck his wicket (rather than if the ball pitches in a line between the wickets, which militates against the old round-arm bowling round the wicket), may or may not prove advisable. It is not a really radical reform.

But far the best change, the most potent, and in every way most profitable to all, to the bowler, the wicket-keep, the fielder, the spectator, and even ultimately to the batsman, would be an improvement in fielding. Some time ago one of the greatest of all cover-points past or present remarked to a friend of his, "If you and I were there, that side would have been out by now." With this man at cover, the batsman was never let off at cover. With a team of such fielders, the game would be quite altered. A century would then mean something. As it is, a player is said to have given no chances when with a field full of Vernon Royles[13] he would have given several chances of being caught, and many chances of being run out. But how can fielding be improved?

Why are there so few prizes for fielding? Why in athletic sports is there a prize only for distance-throwing, and not for regulated direction or regulated pitch? Here is a great opening for schools, and especially to-day when, as Abel said, stone-throwing in cities is sadly discouraged! The beach of the sea-side is not always accessible. Besides this, it is good to practise catching and fielding with a soft ball against a wall; various games of catching and fielding can be made exciting enough; the stump-game (suggested in another chapter) can be adapted to throwing as well as to bowling; points may be counted. Excellent exercise can thus be had at odd moments. Or Fives and left-handed Squash will develop the left side, and prizes for left-hand throwing may be offered by schools. Boxing is capital in its effects on alertness and "eye." There should be boxing by all means.

And let there be training in general--for how can one field well unless he be fresh and untired? Let there be full control of arms and legs and body without loss of balance, full quick stretchings, full and quick stoopings, in all directions; let there be--we repeat--plenty of Fives for the left side and for stooping; diving and swimming for endurance; and the fast extension-movements, at the end of which the extensions should be held for a moment or two.

This implies careful analysis of the mechanisms of fielding--of starting, of catching, of picking up, of throwing in. It implies a *system or systems* based on this analysis. It implies careful study. But if Cricket be a desirable game, above all if it be compulsory, then it must be taught well, especially at the outset. As Murdoch says: "A good ground-work must be laid down, and the young beginner cannot be too painstaking and careful." The drill must not be in all the refinements of Cricket, such as the Ranjiglide; it must be in that A B C of fielding, etc., which no really great fielder has lacked. That which is not by nature must come by art. Some drill there must be, even if it only be self-drill. But drill itself will do a boy no harm to-day. A veteran cricketer, in his time an excellent field and now a superintendent of a boys' institution, tells me on the one hand of the inferiority of fielding to-day, and on the other hand of the lack of persistent concentration among boys to-day. Boys, he says, lack that power, and drill can give it to them so that it lasts through life.

Reform in Cricket must not be merely reform for a few match-players. Apart from increased power of sustained self-control, of immediate self-direction, apart from confidence and readiness, it must be for the greater enjoyment and greater skill of the majority of British boys and men. With this end in view, we may have to adapt Cricket to indoor play in well-lighted and well-ventilated rooms in cities and suburbs (in America the city-clubs, built storey upon storey upwards, allow of other games by electric light). Any old room would do. We do not want *only* this adapted game, any more than we want *only* drill and practice; we want net-play also; practice-games also; matches also. But we want the game itself, the grand old game, when it *is* played, to be played better and to be played better all round, in all its branches, by all its players.

When we come to look at the matter impartially, and to ask what Cricket might and should do for us physically, aesthetically, mentally, morally, as individuals, as groups, as a nation; when we come to compare its effects--even as they now are--with those of our school-lessons in Latin grammar, geography, history, arithmetic, and so on, we do not hesitate to say that Government support is needed, not only in establishing such clubs, for evening and wet-day play within cities, but also for allowing Cricket--the trinity of Cricket, batting and bowling and fielding, and perhaps the theory of Cricket also--to count something in certain Government examinations, especially in those for the Indian Civil Service. For is it not of more value than many crammings?

Let Cricket be given its proper place--no higher, no lower. It is an amusement; true. But it is also an education for character and life. It might be ten times the education that it is, for almost the whole of character and life. Sensible reforms would make it so--reforms which would in no way interfere with Cricket as it is now played in important matches, and as it is now practised in practice-games and at nets. The reforms would prepare for these excellent occasions, and would also serve as substitutes for them and as supplements to them, and would thus bring in many converts to the game, bring back many renegades, and enable Cricket to hold her own against all her rivals, especially against excessive Cycling, Golf, Croquet, Ping-Pong, idleness, the public-house, and that evil for which at present there exists no other name but smuggishness.

THE END

Printed in Dunstable, United Kingdom

63994702R00082